OF POLITICS
& ECONOMICS

OF POLITICS & ECONOMICS

The School of Hard Knocks
and Gentle Persuasion

Steven I. Platt

RAMSES HOUSE PUBLISHING LLC
BALTIMORE, MD

OF POLITICS & ECONOMICS: The School of Hard Knocks and Gentle Persuasion
Copyright © 2023 The Platt Group Inc.

Published by Ramses House Publishing LLC, Baltimore, MD,
www.publishingforlawyers.com

First Printing, 2023
ISBN 978-1-7351462-1-8 paper; 10-digit: 1-7351462-1-8
ISBN 978-1-7351462-4-9 ePub

Notice: The book is written for attorneys, scholars, and laypeople who are interested in historical accounts, opinion, and analysis of economics, law, and politics on a local and federal level.

Library of Congress Control No.: 2022923044

Printed and bound in the United States of America

DISCLAIMER: The opinions expressed herein are solely the author's opinions and are based on his personal experience. The information contained in this book is provided for informational purposes only, and should not be construed as legal advice on any matter. The trans-mission and receipt of information, in whole or in part, via the Internet or through e-mail does not constitute or create a lawyer-client relationship.

The Platt Group Inc.
P.O. Box 6604
Annapolis, MD 21401

*With my deepest love, appreciation, and affection to
my expanded family; each of you has enriched
my life more than you will ever know
in your own unique ways.*

*To my son, Jason Benjamin Platt, and his wife, Anne
Fleetwood Platt; my daughter, Sarah Edan Carter, her
husband, Kevin Carter, and my cherished grandchildren, Dylan Emerson Carter, Benjamin Graham Platt,
and Charlie Robert Platt.*

*To my partner and "Significant Other" going on 20
years, Frances Hughes Glendening.*

*To my ex-wife, Patti Hartlove Platt, for the years she
partnered with me, raised our children, and gave me
the time to live the kind of life that allowed me
to think about and learn the intersection of
law, politics, and economics.*

*To the memory of my parents, Nathan and Adele Platt,
my grandfather, Charlie Platt, and my grandmother,
Rose Platt, whose voyage on stowage from Russia
to Ellis Island in 1913 laid the foundation for me to
live out their and my dreams.*

*My parents raised me to believe I could do anything
that I wanted, limited only by my own capabilities.
This book is the evidence that I believed them.*

OF POLITICS & ECONOMICS
The School of Hard Knocks & Gentle Persuasion

PART ONE: POLITICS 101

PART TWO: ADVANCED GOVERNING

PART THREE: POLITICAL ECONOMICS (GRADUATE LEVEL)

Acknowledgments

I thank the persons who have made this possible by working with me to edit and print these blog posts and columns throughout the years and now to publish them in book form. They include my selfless, trusted, and dependable administrative assistant, Penny M. Simpson, and, of course, my publisher, Tatia Gordon-Troy, Esquire, and her publishing company, Ramses House Publishing, LLC.

I want to remember and thank the deceased friends and mentors who helped shape me and my career. The first mentor I'll mention is Maryland District Court Chief Judge Robert F. Sweeney, whose style, history, and career served as an inspiration and a role model for me. The second is Seventh Circuit Chief Judge Ernest A. Loveless, Jr. for whom I clerked and whose political, diplomatic, and interpersonal skills instructed my conduct for the rest of my life. The third is Court of Appeals Judge Howard S. Chasanow, and the fourth is Peter F. O'Malley, Esquire, who showed me through his example that honesty and integrity can be successfully reconciled with being an effective political and business operative.

I also thank for being my professional colleagues, now retired and good friends still: Judge Glenn T. Harrell, Jr.; Judge William B. Spellbring, Jr.; Judge C. Phillip Nichols, Jr.; Judge Larnzell Martin, Jr.; Judge Leo E. Green; Judge Theresa Nolan; Judge Paul Bowman; Judge Julia Weatherly; and William F. Edwards, Esquire.

About the Author

My first stirring of interest in politics was when I was 15 years old and was confronted with the assassination of President John F. Kennedy. I reacted emotionally. I was in high school at a private military college preparatory school named Massanutten Military Academy, located in the heart of the Shenandoah Valley of Virginia in a little town named Woodstock, about 10 miles from my home of Strasburg, Virginia.

My family members were all Republicans. My grandfather had registered as a Republican, being convinced at the time that he owed allegiance to that party after emigrating from Russia and becoming a naturalized citizen during the then-Republican administration of President Theodore Roosevelt. My father, his only child, followed suit; and the women, my grandmother and later my mother, when they were allowed to register to vote, followed the patriarch of the family.

I, however, having been born on New Year's Day, January 1, 1947, and thereby a certified "Baby Boomer," with my childhood occurring during the 1950s and 1960s, I gravitated toward the vision, promise, philosophy, and style of the young, handsome President John F. Kennedy and the inspiration, a/k/a "Camelot," that he instilled in my generation. The differences of opinion on political issues and the resulting "discussions" at the dinner table with my family were, to say the least, interesting if not always enlightening.

From there, I read, listened, and thought about politics a lot, which led me to become involved in the political campaigns of John V. Lindsay for mayor of New York City, Robert F. Kennedy for U.S. Senate in New York in 1966 followed by his bid for president in 1968, and William Battle for governor of Virginia, all while I was a student at the University of Virginia in Charlottesville, majoring in, you guessed it: Government and Politics.

After a brief stint on active duty with the Maryland National Guard, I moved on to law school at The American University in Washington, D.C. I became further involved in my adopted state of Maryland's local politics, first in the management of a state and county political campaign (1970–71) and again in 1974 in Prince George's County, Maryland. I also served in Annapolis, Maryland, for two years (1971–73) as administrative-legislative assistant to then–state Senator Steny H. Hoyer, who has been a U.S. congressman since 1981 and currently serves as majority leader of The House of Representatives.

During those years, I got a good look at the profession and practices of politics at the federal, state, and local levels. That experience included managing and observing campaigns at every level and observing the practical effects of economics, power, and influence in politics.

It was not until 1973–75, however, that I was able to gain initial insights into what I already had observed: the intersection of politics and economics with the law. During this time is when I was fortunate enough to serve as law clerk to Prince George's County Circuit Court Chief Judge Ernest A. Loveless, Jr. of the Seventh Judicial Circuit of Maryland.

In 1976, I departed the comfort and security of the chamber of Chief Judge Loveless, Jr. to engage in law practice, including a stint as counsel to the Maryland Democratic Party, and chairmanship of the Prince George's County Human Relations Commission (1976–78). That was followed by my election to two four-year terms on The Orphans Court (Probate Court) for Prince George's County (1978–86).

In 1986, I was honored to be appointed by Governor Harry R. Hughes to serve on the Bench of The District Court of Maryland. I was further honored to be elevated to the Bench of The Circuit Court of Maryland by Governor William Donald Schaefer, where I served until 2007.

Finally, in 2007, I left the full-time Judicial Bench to enter the very different world of "alternative dispute resolution" or ADR. I also began my "Pursuit of Justice" blog during this period, and am still going strong to this day. The world of ADR has provided me with the opportunity to work in private dispute resolution system and design, conflict coaching, and consulting.

Such has been my personal and professional trajectory. These opinions represent the product of my journey to date. My limited hope, if not expectation, is that these opinions will motivate readers to examine their own opinions.

A 50-Year Addiction
and a Never-ending Pursuit

"These warts are all unapologetically mine."

Are you a "political junkie"? If so, you're in the right place. *Of Politics & Economics: The School of Hard Knocks & Gentle Persuasion* is for attorneys, scholars, and anyone interested in historical accounts, opinion, and analysis of economics, law, and politics on a local, state, and federal level—according to *yours truly*.

I am a self-proclaimed political junkie who has had the pleasure of thinking, talking, and writing on these topics for the better part of 50 years. This book, however, covers only the last 13 years or so during my time as a columnist for *The Daily Record* in Baltimore and as a blogger under the theme, "A Pursuit of Justice: The Intersection of Law, Economics, and Politics."

In late 2006, I started that blog, which I had hoped to contemporaneously develop into an op/ed. column. My relationship with the newspaper provided me an opportunity to think and write about the things that have mattered to me the most for the better part of my adult life—law, economics, and politics—with the exception of my family.

I do not suffer from any misconception that law, economics, and politics are what matters to everyone, or that they should. This addiction is mine, and mine alone, to bear. It has occupied my mind and directed my pen as a political activist, staffer, operator, lawyer, and judge on three different courts, and now as a private mediator, arbitrator, conflict coach, consultant, and op/ed. columnist/blogger.

The pursuit of justice at the intersection of law, economics, and politics is still ongoing. The path memorialized in these pages, I believe, will lead readers to where justice will be found, if it exists, perhaps partially obscured by signs reading "Under Construction–Slow Down."

The thoughts, opinions, and, I dare say, political and cultural analytics derived from my journey, while not describing the journey itself, chronicles my *Daily Record* columns, blog posts, legal opinions, speeches, and other print media coverage over the last 30 years.

The pieces primarily remain untouched from when they were first published whether 13 years ago or a few months ago. They also are in no particular order, but for the specific sections in which they appear.

These warts are all *unapologetically* mine. Hopefully, you will enjoy reading them and they will stimulate your own critical thinking on these subjects.

As my father would tell me with some frequency, "You can learn from anybody." As I would find out in my life's journey, my father was wrong! You can learn from *almost* anybody, not all. Nevertheless, I recommend listening to everybody. You never know—you might learn something.

PART ONE

Politics 101

Chapter 1

Is Politics Corrupt? Stay Tuned to Your Supreme Court Station

""[T]he line is blurry between the exercise of constitutional rights and the commission of a crime."

Good news! The Supreme Court of the United States has finally agreed to define the term "corruption." That term has been used to label pejoratively what columnist George Will and others have correctly observed that which is the undeniable fact—"politics in our representative democracy is transactional."

In granting former Virginia Governor Robert McDonnell's petition for a writ of certiorari in 2015 in the case that resulted in his conviction in federal court, the highest Court in the land, after inexplicably turning down several previous opportunities to do so, has agreed to resolve the conflict between several federal circuit courts of appeals.

The issue on which those circuit courts have split is what evidence is required to establish criminal intent when an elected official is prosecuted for accepting political and/or personal contributions and then taking some action—even making some gesture or simply providing more than routine ordinary access to him- or herself or his or her subordinate government officials—arguably in return for that contribution.

The context for this issue being brought forward for judicial determination are the convictions of former Virginia Governor Robert McDonnell and his now estranged wife, former First Lady Maureen McDonnell, for accepting gifts from a former "friend" and the friend's company.

These gifts included six-figure business and personal "loans," shopping trips, and partial payment for a daughter's wedding reception. Thereafter, the governor bestowed a gubernatorial blessing in various forms of the friend's company's product (vitamin supplements) as well as increased access to certain government officials and facilities.

The question that the Supreme Court hopefully will address is, was this "quid pro quo corruption?" A federal jury believed it was based on instructions on the applicable law by a U.S. district court judge who reviewed the jury's verdict and agreed with it. A unanimous panel of the U.S. Court of Appeals for the Fourth Circuit affirmed the lower court's decision and refused to reconsider that decision. Nevertheless, other federal circuits have taken a different view.

One federal circuit court has held that to establish the *mens rea* (criminal intent) necessary for a conviction, "an explicit promise" is required to be proven. The *Oxford English Dictionary* defines "explicit" as "stated clearly and in detail leaving no room for confusion or doubt."

Another federal circuit court, however, has held that "explicit" does not mean an "express or an actually and clearly stated promise that a particular "official" action will be exchanged for a contribution. This far less rigorous standard holds that explicit "quid pro quo" can mean only a "state of mind inferred from perhaps suspicious circumstances."

This opens the breadth of prosecutorial discretion dangerously beyond the other standard. More importantly, it would in the opinion of this writer tempt zealous prosecutors and perhaps judges and juries to ascribe unspoken but criminal mental states to elected officials who are already held in low esteem generally.

In a nutshell, the problem that the U.S. Supreme Court will now attempt to address is, as George Will has stated, "the line is blurry between the exercise of constitutional rights and the commission of a crime." For example, as one commentator asked with reference to the McDonnell case, is showing up at a reception for the launch of a product by itself a quid pro quo? If so, is President Barack Obama, after accepting a campaign contribution from DreamWorks movie company or its owner prohibited from going to a Democratic Party fundraiser hosted by DreamWorks and its owner in Hollywood and saying nice things about DreamWorks Company?

As another example, is the very common practice of governors in states with strong gubernatorial offices, including Maryland, to not provide funds in a supplemental budget for a project favored by a legislator if he or she doesn't support an unrelated bill or project favored by the governor a criminal violation?

The backdrop for this, and the drama associated with it, is the multiple investigations of the troubles and travails of Governor Chris Christie of New Jersey. Governor Christie's now former deputy chief of staff, as well as his former close friend and political advisor—including officials at the New York/New Jersey Port Authority now banished—have been fired from their positions and relieved of their responsibilities.

In the case of the deputy chief of staff, she appears to have initiated a four-day traffic jam on the George Washington Bridge to punish a mayor for not endorsing the governor's re-election campaign. The governor's friend and advisor is no longer advising Governor Chris Christie officially or unofficially as a result of joking about it despite its victims, including an individual who died because the emergency healthcare he needed couldn't be reached in time as a result of the delay, as well as school children being delayed and people not being able to get to work on time.

The multiple state and federal investigations of this event in New Jersey are now expanding exponentially to include allegations that officials, including New Jersey's lieutenant governor, threatened to withhold federal funds sent to New Jersey for relief of Hurricane Sandy–related damages if the Jersey City mayor and other mayors did not agree to support a development project favored by Governor Christie.

Governor Christie has denied knowledge of any of this. His lieutenant governor has branded the allegations as "illogical" and therefore "inconceivable."

"Illogical"—not really! Inconceivable? Hardly. In fact, as columnist George F. Will has pointed out, well known, honest, and decent candidates routinely solicit the support of interest groups, corporations, wealthy individuals, and such entities regularly solicit the solicitousness of candidates.

It is, therefore, not uncommon for wealthy individuals to support candidates lavishly for elective offices at every level of government with the expectation of receiving in return jobs, ambassadorships, appointments to boards and commissions, and/or with the hope that the candidate, if elected, will show gratitude for their generosity in the form of implementing policies desired by their financial benefactors.

The question remains, is this "quid pro quo corruption"? Until this question is answered directly by the U.S. Supreme Court, honest Americans running for public office risk criminal prosecution because of the wide discretion prosecutors arguably possess to criminalize the financing of their campaigns and careers.

This is the concern if not the complaint voiced by, among others, "Morning Joe" Scarborough in commenting on the McDonnell case. Conversely, in the absence of a bright line limiting a prosecutor's authority, at risk will be convictions obtained by dedicated prosecutors trying to root out and punish corruption by aggressively holding corrupt candidates and their contributors accountable.

This is because it is well-settled constitutional law that fundamental due process is denied when the law does not give proper notice of what kind of behavior is proscribed criminally. It is this notice requirement that circumscribes prosecutorial discretion in corruption cases. This was the reason that the convictions of several high-profile elected officials and corporate officers for "depriving citizens of home services" were overturned on appeal in *Citizens United v. Federal Election Commission* by several federal circuit courts of appeals.

The effect of this blurry line has a long and colorful history in Maryland, which can reference the convictions of two governors, several county executives, as well as state and federal legislators, including most recently the case of an incumbent state senator whose articulated defense to corruption charges was that he was not clever or sophisticated enough to comprehend where the line, blurry as it is, was between quid pro quo and helping his employer and constituent. A jury of honest citizens sympathized and acquitted the senator.

That blurry line needs to be straightened and brightened by the U.S. Supreme Court. It needs to be straightened with a vision of what the Court recognized in *Caperton v. Massey Coal* (556 U.S. 868), but then afterward ignored in *Citizens United v. Federal Election Commission* (558 U.S. 310):

> *Whether after a realistic appraisal of psychological tendencies and human weakness, there is such a 'risk of actual bias of prejudgment by the official' as a result of campaign contributions and other personal and financial arrangements that the practice must be forbidden if the guarantee of due process is to be adequately implemented.*

Chapter 2

Corruption May Explain the Previously Unexplainable

"It is one of the lamentable frailties of mankind that when one's wrong is most grievous, his self-justification is most passionate ..."

Watching and listening to our elected congressmen stumble toward the latest deadline for addressing the immediate "Debt Limit Crisis" by rhetorically scratching and clawing at each other is at best annoying and at worse numbing. That "crisis," like previous crises, generated by the same issue and similar circumstances was created by prior Congresses unnecessarily (unless you believe political and legislative posturing is necessary); but, nevertheless, Congress repeatedly votes to limit by statute the level of our federal government's debt to less than the amount required to operate the government as mandated by the laws that, you guessed it, were passed by Congresses, past and present.

Now, we all know (I think) that if our federal government spends more than it takes in as it has for some time, it must pay for this excess spending with dollars printed and borrowed for that purpose.

If the government already has mandated the spending and/or already purchased goods and services as this country's federal government clearly has done by pledging its heretofore unquestioned full faith and credit, then the people elected to run the government should not ignore that fact or stare blindly at that reality and limit the government's credit line as if it had not already been pledged. If they do, then they can accurately be described as (choose one or more, if applicable) irresponsible, unpatriotic, ignorant, or delusional.

The most charitable description of what has been going on in Washington, D.C., for the last few months is a "principled debate" over the proper method of financing the current debt while we reduce it in the future. Last time I checked, there were two ways to do that—spend less or collect more revenue.

The two are not mutually exclusive; and when your national debt is $14.3 trillion, a compelling argument can be made that "wise political leaders" ought to at least be willing to talk about both ways and not hold hostage the country's full faith and credit that they profess to love in order to satisfy their electoral and financial base's preference for political theater over sensible public policy development and problem-solving legislating.

In an obituary for former Virginia Congressman Richard H. Poff who died in 2011, he was quoted as deeply regretting his previous position in favor of school segregation, which he later repudiated. He explained his previous position by stating,

> *It is one of the lamentable frailties of mankind that when one's wrong is most grievous, his self-justification is most passionate, perhaps in the pitiful hope that the fervor of his self-defense will somehow prove him right.*

That is yet another explanation for the behavior of our elected leaders, which at least holds out the hope that what we're seeing and hearing from them is fleeting and that they will behave better very shortly.

Nevertheless, the current visual of our elected leaders with some notable exceptions on both sides of the aisle pandering to their political and financial bases instead of doing their jobs is not pretty. Nor does the audio sound any better. Why then is our most optimistic scenario for the future limited to hoping that what we're currently experiencing is temporary?

The media at least pretends to search for an explanation whether digitally, on cable television, on the web, and in print. They haven't found it! However, they have begun to focus on corruption whether by happenstance or habit, which is found in every society—whether primitive or advanced as well as across geographic and demographic borders, in both public and private institutions and persons—as at least a partial explanation for what appears to be irresponsible or even irrational behavior.

Corruption, which diminishes public trust and confidence in political leaders, government officials, business and labor leaders, party officials, even the media itself (witness Rupert Murdoch's recent problems), is increasingly visible as a result of the internet.

Corruption is increasingly noticeable in every continent and country as well as international organizations. From Communist China through the emerging economies in Africa, Asia, and Latin America to the United States and the United Kingdom, corruption is examined and scrutinized in a way that is often unwelcomed by the business and political elites who are the targets of the media's focus.

The form and nature of corruption emerging in the 21st century and its relationship to our leaders' behavior will be explored in future columns—hopefully after they figure out how to maintain our country's full faith and credit.

Chapter 3

Corruption Precipitates Crisis in Confidence

*"Democracy is the theory that the common people
know what they want and deserve to get it—
good and hard."*

You have to be a "political junkie," which I apparently am, when you sit, as I often do, on many Sunday mornings watching "The Talks." Having provided the evidence of my condition, I hereby admit to it and the fantasies that accompany it.

One of those fantasies is that I will hear and thereby learn something new or profound from either the "guests" or the "talking heads" who inhabit the "expert panels" that appear in the second half of these hour-long shows for the stated purpose of commenting on what the "guests," who were interviewed on the first half of the program, said and the news of the past week generally.

Well, so far it hasn't happened. Nevertheless, there is no doubt that I will continue to occupy my Sunday mornings more often than not by watching these programs in the hope that I will be more "enlightened" after watching them. Further commenting in the context established by newly minted presidential candidate Texas Governor Rick Perry, I do not consider it "treasonous" to do so.

What I have heard and read repeatedly, not just on Sunday mornings but virtually every day, are politicians and pundits, alike, lamenting the inability of our political leaders and/or the U.S. political system to manage the national, indeed, international economic crises that we find ourselves in. Unfortunately, that lament has spread beyond the politicians and pundits to one of our credit rating agencies, Standard & Poor's, which has produced very tangible damage to at least our national psyche, if not our economy, by lowering our national credit rating from AAA to AA+.

In wreaking that havoc on our previously sterling credit rating and the unshakable confidence in our government that it historically justified at home and abroad, Standard & Poor's set forth the reason for its action:

> *The downgrade reflects our view that the effectiveness, stability and predictability of American policymaking and political institutions have weakened at a time of ongoing fiscal and economic challenges.*

The question, then, is why have American policymaking and political institutions weakened? Nationally recognized politicians and pundits have Sunday morning talk shows, cable and digital news, newspapers and magazines on which to offer their respective answers to that question.

One explanation, "the polarization of the system," begs the same question stated another way—why has the system become so permanently polarized that it is arguably dysfunctional at this point in our nation's history? The suggested responses to that pointed inquiry include "political amnesia," "our under-regulated campaign finance system," as well as the anger and intensity of both the political class (over ideological things) and the public (over values).

Well, let me offer my one-word explanation for this phenomenon: "Corruption."

I proffer this explanation as a retired state court judge, who before going on the Bench full time in 1986 was heavily involved in and observed politics (managing campaigns) at all levels of government for almost 20 years.

Even thereafter, while on three different Maryland state court Benches, I continued to observe with some insight the political scene while repressing any and all partisan thought that might have surfaced if I was not a member of this state's judiciary.

"Corruption" is variously defined. *Webster's Third New International Dictionary* defines it as the "impairment of integrity, virtue, or moral principal" or alternatively the "inducement (as of a political official) by means of improper consideration to commit a violation of duty."

Interestingly and more to the point, *Black's Law Dictionary* defines "corruption" as "an act done with intent to give some advantage inconsistent with official duty and the rights of others."

Applying these definitions, the evidence of "corruption" at every level of government and society is widespread, pervasive, and deep. Within the last few years in Maryland, we have seen it in its crudest form at the county and city levels with the conviction of a former mayor of Baltimore, the pleas of guilty by a former county executive and his spouse, an elected county councilwoman in Prince George's County, as well as the indictment for corrupt campaign practices of key campaign aides to a former Maryland governor. We have also watched the scandal that threatened to envelop the new mayor of Washington, D.C.

Nationally and internationally, corruption is more subtle but nonetheless not that difficult to detect. Daniel Kaufman, a senior fellow at the Brookings Institute, observes "overly cozy relationships among elites in Western societies that are ethically dangerous even when they do not involve outright criminality."

These "unhealthy links" between power, the media, and money, writes Peter Apps, whose title ironically is "Political Risk Correspondent" for Reuters, "may be politically explosive as societies become more unequal due to financial and economic crisis" citing the scandal involving Rupert Murdoch's media holdings, the British government, and Scotland Yard.

That "explosion" may, in fact, be occurring in our country while this column is written as evidenced by what has been described as "Change Elections" at the federal level in 2006, 2008, and 2010.

We can reduce "corruption," but because we're human, we can't eliminate it. In the meantime, in 2011, as we reflect on how we got where we are, subject to further analysis, I suggest we remember what H.L. Mencken said—which may be the simplest yet clearest explanation of our current plight:

> *Democracy is the theory that the common people know what they want and deserve to get it—good and hard.*

Chapter 4

What's Wrong with Our Broken Political Process?

"Well, it ain't necessarily so."

It is 2011, and the Congress of the United States is on a "break" while the federal government faces the possibility of a "shutdown" in less than a week if the seemingly irreconcilable and mostly newly elected "Tea Party" conservative Republicans can't find common ground, at least temporarily, with enough mostly liberal Democrats "left over" from the last election.

Talk about fiddling while Rome burns.

Meanwhile, in the heartland of our great country, Wisconsin is witnessing its body politic vaporize in the form of the Democratic minority of its state legislators fleeing to its political sanctuary in the state of Illinois in order to stymie the Republican majority's effort to legislatively curtail the collective-bargaining rights of certain Wisconsin public employees.

This occurs while demonstrators on both sides of the issue crowd the public square in the state capital of Madison with signs and speeches impugning the intelligence, integrity, and decency of Governor Scott Walker and his ideological opponents, including President Barack Obama and his political organization, which has been called out to both enhance and rally the pro-union numbers in the crowds.

All of this takes place while most states that are required to pass balanced budgets are addressing fiscal issues generated by "structural deficits," which vary from potentially catastrophic (*e.g.*, California, Wisconsin, New York, and Illinois), to merely serious (*e.g.*, Maryland) without the luxury of being able to print money even temporarily to address them.

This limitation leads the elected leaders in these states to propose "structural solutions," such as restricting or eliminating the rights of public employees to collectively bargain for more and more tax dollars to pay for future benefits and salaries.

When these elected leaders make these proposals, which by definition are neither short-term nor solely economic, they are usually described as "draconian" by the representatives of those citizens whose quality of life and rights are most directly affected. From there, the rhetoric usually heads further south as their plight is dramatized even without any context that would clarify the reality-based choices generated, in part, by elections—rhetoric that has consequences.

"Well, it ain't necessarily so," say two fellow mediators who have written a book of less than 200 pages entitled, *The Cure for Broken Political Process*. Coauthor Sol Erdman is president of the Center for Collaborative Democracy, which he describes as "a non-profit, non-partisan organization that has developed innovative ways for citizens and politicians to resolve ideological conflicts." Coauthor Lawrence Susskind is director of the MIT-Harvard Public Disputes Program. He has mediated national policy debates, refereed regional political battles, and helped negotiate international treaties—including the Kyoto Protocol on global warming.

Their insights into conflict resolution and its role in our representative democracy result from mediating among warring interest groups, government agencies, businesses, communities, and even nations.

These adversaries, the authors point out, started out angrier than typical politicians. Examples cited include the work of the Council on the Sustainable Development (CSD) appointed by President Bill Clinton in 1993. It included the CEOs of Chevron Oil, Pacific Gas & Electric, S.C. Johnson, Ciba Geigy, and Georgia-Pacific sitting at the same table and staring across it at the leaders of the Sierra Club, the Environmental Defense Fund, and the Natural Resources Defense Fund.

Also interspersed among these long-standing enemies were the head of the Environmental Protection Agency (EPA) and the secretaries of Interior, Commerce, and Energy. Some at this table had regularly impugned the others' motives, patriotism, and honesty. Many were suing each other.

To make a long story short, the process was not simple, nor was it easy. Hostility and suspicion dominated early on. But all had one thing in common—they did not want to keep spending time and money warring. So they agreed to keep meeting for over two years.

By February 1996, all 25 members of the CSD had agreed on how to make major progress on the key environmental questions of that time. Furthermore, they spelled out the details in a 185-page report. That report was endorsed by nearly every major environmental group as well as almost all relevant industry associations, labor unions, and government agencies.

Why then was the report ignored by both Democrats and Republicans? The answer the authors suggest is "'the environment' is apparently too good a campaign issue to lose to a mere solution."

Other examples cited directly from the authors' experience include how the National Commission on Retirement Policy's unanimous recommendations to best meet everyone's needs in retirement and save Social Security were completely ignored by Democrats and Republicans in Congress and by the president—a pattern that repeated itself in 2004 when the National Commission on Energy Policy (NCEP), consisting of 16 corporate CEOs, environmental leaders, academics, and former government officials, agreed unanimously on how America could best meet its ravenous need for energy.

The NCEP issued a 148-page report explaining how to cut our consumption of oil, reduce foreign imports, and slow down global warming—all at minimal cost. That, too, was ignored.

The question then is what is it about these ideological adversaries that enabled them to sit down with each other, negotiate, and solve problems, and why can't politicians learn from them or even emulate them?

This writer's short answer: The right people must be in the room and their mindset must be reality-based.

Chapter 5

Loss of Public Trust and Confidence Caused by Corruption

*"[T]he party has really serious
corruption problems right now."*

Whether your daily routine starts with a complement to your coffee by going to get the newspaper, consulting with online news sources, or both, there are inevitably two themes that leap off the pages of whatever you read—the loss of confidence by the people in their elected and appointed governmental officials and institutions, and perhaps the cause of that lost confidence: "corruption."

Whether you begin with international, national, state, or local news, the pervasiveness of corruption in various forms around the globe is apparent and cuts across all forms and levels of government. It is the subject of extensive coverage in the media regardless of the ownership and control of that media, and it even at times envelops the media outlets themselves—for example, the Rupert Murdoch–owned media empire.

In India, the prime minister attempts to persuade Anna Hazare, "the leader of a nationwide uprising against corruption," to end her hunger strike by proposing "stronger legislation against graft."

Even in authoritarian China, the ruling Chinese Communist Party, while celebrating its 90th anniversary at a time (this summer) boasting 80 million members, acknowledges "the party has really serious corruption problems right now." This party is the largest political party in the world, governing the world's second-largest economy.

This has caused one Chinese communist party official, Chen Baosheng, vice president of the Central Party School and a disciplinary authority, to describe what he characterizes as "a deterioration of beliefs" and to proffer as a cure that "we should strengthen the teaching of morality."

This would hopefully stem the tide of corruption, which has led to the punishment of 146,517 communist party members for "corruption" last year. These included several sensational cases where party officials were alleged to have killed their mistresses to silence them, as well as embezzled large-scale kickbacks and misappropriated government expenses for their personal use.

In the western hemisphere in Central and South America, Brazilian President Dilma Rousseff, whom *The Economist*, a British news magazine, reports, "arrived in the presidential palace with a reputation as a no-nonsense manager," has found herself "sucked into the political swamp that is Brasilia." According to *The Economist*:

> *She has reacted firmly and correctly to corruption scandals. Her reward has been signs of mutiny and disillusionment in her ramshackle political coalition whose smaller members are interested only in jobs and money for personal gain or party financing.*

Similar issues are noticeable in Argentina, headed by President Christina Fernandez, and in the upcoming election in our neighbor to the south, Mexico, where another woman, Josefina Vazquez Mota, may emerge as the strongest candidate of the ruling National Action Party (PAN) based on her credentials as the "Social Development

Minister who cleared out incompetent officials" under former President Vicente Fox.

Why all of these countries are turning to women to fight corruption will not be the subject of this column, but perhaps should be explored later, when the opportunity presents itself. It is at the moment certainly worthy of at least this preliminary notice.

It is a trend that this writer is sure will be encouraged within the campaigns of the two female Republican women who are most heavily into the 2012 presidential campaign—Michelle Bachman (R. Minn.), who is an announced candidate, and former Republican vice presidential candidate Alaska Governor Sarah Palin, who continues to tease her followers with speeches and appearances designed to keep their interest in her as a prospective presidential candidate besides making her a lot of money and getting her the attention that she so obviously seeks and enjoys without accountability.

Both Representative Bachman and Governor Palin have incorporated the latest fashionable rhetorical shot at corruption into their standard speeches more than any of the other candidates. They have done so by repeatedly using the phrase, "crony capitalism," mostly with reference to the alleged practices of Governor Rick Perry of Texas, the frontrunner for the Republican nomination (Bachman's focus), but also to pejoratively label government involvement in the economy generally (Palin's focus).

This phrase "crony capitalism" has not yet been defined by either of these candidates. I will, therefore, suggest that Katie Couric be recalled to ask both of them what it means and that neither candidate be permitted to use the phrase again until she has responded to Couric's inquiry with an answer that is coherent and consistent with well-settled principles of law and economics.

Whether Representative Bachman or Governor Palin can define "crony capitalism" or not, this column in the future will explore what it means to our democracy and to the beneficiaries of the public and private partnerships in our mixed economy that have thrived without objection from either political party until recently.

Chapter 6

Destructive Partisanship March Can Be Halted

*"It is often easier to fight for principles
than to live up to them."*

Destructive partisanship in our politics will continue its march and will alternatively deter or consume many of our best and brightest unless we elect and appoint more true partisans.

Yes, you read that correctly.

We need more true partisans in government who genuinely want to advance the causes they claim to stand for, not just posture and bicker about them for public consumption and their own political posterity.

Those who want to posture and bicker to gain public approval are demonstrably not true partisans because the constituency they respond to most consistently is the combination of the loud inner voices of their own personal insecurities, coupled with the surface noise of the vocal interest groups, citizens, and demanding talk show hosts that feed on the need of these weak leaders for partisan approval.

These weak leaders have neither the strength of character nor the trust and confidence of the people whom they claim to represent. Both are necessary to negotiate with true partisans on the other side of an issue. Lacking that essential level of confidence in their own ability as well as the trust of their partisan constituents—both of which are necessary to effectively negotiate with their adversaries on any important and complex issue—they inevitably choose not to seriously engage in difficult, intense, and often-long substantive negotiations, all the while blaming the lack of progress on these issues on "excessive partisanship" and on their ideological adversaries having "too much power and influence."

This so-called "explanation" actually explains nothing. Competing ideas, strong interest groups, and demanding citizens are not the problem—our country's history illustrates that many times over, starting with the framers of our Declaration of Independence and our Constitution. Each of the framers fought for the most powerful interests in his home state. They also waged fierce ideological battles.

The difference is as fellow mediators Sol Erdman, president of the Center for Collaborative Democracy, and Lawrence Susskind, director of the MIT and Harvard Public Disputes Resolution Program, point out in their book, *The Cure for Broken Political Process*, that those leaders knew that if they genuinely wanted to advance the causes they claimed to stand for, they would have to negotiate enduring agreements with their ideological opposites; and they did.

Furthermore, unlike so many of their more timid successors today, they had the courage to do so. That courage emanated from their innate confidence in their own ability to articulate the basis for their negotiating position to their partisan constituents and to convince them of the wisdom of moving their cause forward in the only way possible in a representative democracy—negotiation.

When leaders do this, as is illustrated throughout not only our history but world history, they effectively tie their personal and political future to their success in convincing their constituents that they have gotten everything they could for them and that the agreement reached is fair, responsible, and—most importantly—in their interest.

In order to do that, these leaders have to come to the table with the basic trust and confidence of their own constituents.

In other words, we have to choose the right leaders.

Perhaps the classic illustration of that most important proposition is the example cited by Sol Erdman and Lawrence Susskind: The repeal of Apartheid in South Africa.

> *What made it happen were the two negotiators: FW. De Klerk and Nelson Mandela, South Africa's white supremacist prime minister meeting face-to-face with hero of most black South Africans.*
>
> *Both men knew that if they struck a deal that made sense to them, each one could sell it to his own camp, which they did. De Klerk persuaded most whites that they had to make peace with the ever more militant black majority. Meanwhile, Mandela convinced most blacks that to gain equality, they had to guarantee the then-entrenched white minority some power in future governments. Who else could have negotiated a deal that nearly every South African would abide by?*

So how do we choose the right leaders? Erdman and Susskind suggest that we start by recognizing that there are a handful of people who have a high public profile on any large issue, which brings heightened and widespread credibility. We bring them together. Everyone accepts the reality that every negotiator is pulled in two directions. As Erdman and Susskind point out:

> *Each one wants the most benefits for his or her own side yet each one wants the other parties to contribute toward a solution. And to make that happen, a negotiator has to cooperate with his supposed enemies. Nearly every representative struggles to find the right balance between cooperating with his or her opponents and grabbing all he can for his own camp.*

How does a negotiator determine what constitutes the "right balance"? Erdman and Susskind acknowledge there's no "magic formula" and then follow with a further suggestion, which reveals their profession and the bias that accompanies it. They suggest that a neutral facilitator run all the meetings. The neutral facilitator or mediator can then "coax anyone who gets too demanding." That suggests the mediator-facilitator would use the "facilitative" or even a subtly "evaluative" technique of mediation.

Does this guarantee that a deal will result? No, but it beats the alternative we watch on the news every day, and it illustrates what two very diverse political figures of the second-half of the last century poignantly noted based on their very different history and constituents.

Adlai Stevenson in 1952 said:

> *It is often easier to fight for principles than to live up to them.*

Perhaps that is because as Ronald Reagan noted some 32 years later on April 11, 1984:

> *I've always believed that a lot of trouble in the world would disappear if we were talking to each other instead of about each other.*

Chapter 7

Midnight in Paris for Politicians

"It is difficult to get a man to understand something when his salary depends on his not understanding it."

On Saturday evening, June 25, 2011, in a Bethesda, Maryland, movie theatre, I witnessed what one reviewer described as "the return of Woody Allen to at least one of his beloved forms" in the direction of his new movie, *Midnight in Paris*.

The story, which one capsule review suggests, creates a "larky slightly tart and altogether bountiful mood" and tells the story of a "would-be serious author" visiting Paris in 2010 (whom I naturally identify with since I started writing this column).

There, while he enjoys Parisian wine to arguable excess, he is transformed back to the Paris of the 1920s where he engages in and observes conversations between his heroes and heroines, writers, and artists of that era: F. Scott Fitzgerald, and his wife, Zelda; Ernest Hemingway; Gertrude Stein; Pablo Picasso; and Paul Gauguin. The conversations between these characters, based on caricatures of their earlier-life progenitors trading barbs between dry martinis and their favorite wines, bring to life the ironies of all of our human existences.

My favorite exchange occurs when the lead character, "Gil," portrayed by Owen Wilson, asks the famed author and critic, Gertrude Stein, to read and critique the book he is writing to establish himself as a serious writer in lieu of his current professional life as a well-salaried "script writer" in Hollywood. She does so and later encourages him to keep at it, because it is the important job of a novelist to relieve his readers of their boredom with the routine of their daily existence.

Gil's reflection on Gertrude Stein's advice, and his subsequent determination to risk his ability to earn a future economic livelihood as well as forego his plans to wed a woman with little imagination or interest in his work to be a serious writer, got me thinking. I thought about whether that very basic human desire to relieve ourselves of our own boredom with the routine of our daily existences is motivating the problems that we are having in our political life.

The political class, in particular, seems to be prone to this very human desire to lead (1) an interesting and (2) meaningful, personal, and professional life and to equate doing so with holding public office. For this reason as *New York Times* magazine writer Matt Bai has pointed out:

> *The political system is imperiled mostly because too many of our politicians just can't seem to imagine any worse fate in life than losing an election.*

This phenomenon is not necessarily to be expected in the 21st century. In fact, the members of the political class, who seem almost universally susceptible to it, are missing what Matt Bai articulates and those particularly younger members of the newly "flattened world" experience on a daily basis—"the modern ethos of career adventurism." That "career adventurism" experience almost inevitably entails—for the children of the millennium and even the younger "Baby Boomers"—cycling or shifting through a succession of jobs during their professional lives.

This is unlike their parents who may have worked at the same firm or factory for 30 years or more and have a pension, Social Security, and Medicare into which they contributed to show for it. These mostly younger professionals and workers at best have a 401K. Many do not expect to have Social Security and/or Medicare "as we know it."

This is in stark contrast to many of our politicians who still cling to their offices at almost any cost to conscience or constituency, as if they could not bear to even think about holding another job. Matt Bai points out:

> it is this outmoded sense of entitlement" that lobbyists, the media, and other sources of "outside pressure exploit to pray on politicians' insecurities about their ability to hold on to the only part of their daily routine that makes their lives interesting and fulfilling.

The problem then is not with the lobbyists, the media, or the proliferation of money in politics. The problem is with the people whom we are electing and appointing who simply choose far too often not to do what they know is right and face the possible political consequences of their actions.

The standard we hold these people to should certainly be no lower than any other occupation. Most of us would not knowingly harm or defraud our clients or customers just because we were ordered by our boss to do so even at the risk of losing our job. Admittedly, federal and state legislators don't face moral dilemmas this stark. But they are required to choose constantly between the welfare of their constituents and their own self-preservation politically.

The question we should answer is whether it is really so outside the bounds of human nature to expect politicians to serve the interests of the people who elect them even when their own re-elections are at risk? Most of the time, politicians understand what the right thing to do is or they choose not to understand it.

This writer thinks it is not unreasonable to expect politicians to understand and do the right thing, although as Upton Sinclair said way back in 1935:

> It is difficult to get a man to understand something when his salary depends on his not understanding it.

Our politicians don't need to be rescued by public financing, stricter regulation of lobbying and lobbyists, or other systemic remedies that may be legislated. They just need to go to the movies and see *Midnight in Paris*. Then, they need to think about the movie they just saw with a view toward putting their lives and careers in perspective.

Chapter 8

Trump-Speak vs. Candidate-Speak

*"Don't worry about it. Look what I've done—built
huge, impressive buildings, made great deals,
and enriched myself in the process
by outsmarting other people ..."*

Donald Trump has clearly taken political theater to a new level; and the mainstream media, not to mention social media, can't resist the temptation to give him their almost undivided attention and thereby encourage and enable him to take it even further.

I have previously written about the dangers of allowing political theater to drive public policy, inadvertently or otherwise. This year, we are witnessing political theater being substituted for policy development with no regrets or apologies.

Donald Trump is, of course, leading the way with his off-the-cuff rhetoric and "tweets" tailored to the events and/or headlines of the day and the desire to "hit back hard" at whoever annoyed him or his followers the previous day or even that morning. He could be taking aim at one of the other candidates or even a media person, such as Megyn Kelly, who is an anchor with that well-known liberal outlet, Fox News.

In fact, Trump has on more than one occasion described what he has been doing as "having fun" and "waging war" with one or more of the other candidates. He is clearly enjoying himself at the expense of even a modicum of civility and substance in our political discourse.

In the case of Wisconsin Governor Scott Walker, Trump said that he thought Walker was a "nice man" and he gave Walker money, then Walker criticized him, "so now I can attack him." In the case of Jeb Bush, his basic criticism is that Bush is "low energy" and, therefore, he "can't and won't get anything done."

As far as I can tell, Trump has at least three policy positions: (1) he would round up and deport all 11 million "illegal" immigrants at an unknown, but no doubt prohibitive, cost in dollars, time, and personnel—"They gotta go": (2) he would build a "wall" between Mexico and the United States also at an unknown cost—"Just trust me, I am a builder and I know how to build things"; and (3) he would "police the hell out of the Iran deal."

Trump would also unilaterally defund Planned Parenthood for which he apparently developed strong negative feelings in the last year despite support for them previously.

In short, "The Donald" has as his overarching narrative and political philosophy, "The Art of the Deal," which is the name of his most recent book. His position in a nutshell: "I'm really rich" and "really smart" and all the other candidates, Republican and Democrat, as well as the current President of the United States, his previous Secretary of State, Hillary Rodham Clinton, and the current Secretary of State, John Kerry, are "dumb" and make really "bad deals."

> *But don't worry, I, Donald Trump, am a great businessman who has taken over many bad deals and made them work because I am a great manager of people and money. Therefore, I can do it again. So elect me President of the United States, and in four years, you'll interview me and tell me 'you've done a great job as President, Mr. Trump.'"*

This, as he told *Meet the Press* moderator Chuck Todd.

For doing what he is doing and saying what he has been saying, Donald Trump has been heavily criticized and has been called "irresponsible," "insulting," "dishonest," a "flip flopper," even heaven forbid "not a true conservative" as well as disrespectful of women, Hispanics, and others. But let's be honest: in one way, he has been more candid with the public than all of the other candidates, as well as his critics in the media.

Donald Trump has dramatically injected the culture and ethics of the private world into the world of politics with its unspoken but widely recognized large quantum of hypocrisy and its manifestation in the form of political correctness—the same private world that most of us live and work in as well as the world of Big Business where he has labored during his adult life.

The world of politics and the political class (elites), including all of the other candidates who inhabit it, are obviously having difficulty coping with this unexpected intrusion and disruption of their world. The polls reflect their inability to overcome it or cast it aside. Furthermore, Trump has been totally honest about what he is doing and why.

What he is doing is appealing directly to the desire of what at first appeared to be 10% to 15% of the voters of both political parties, but now looks like as much as 30% to 40% of those voters of both parties to support a candidate who will not only speak to their values, but act on them in a way that convinces them that the candidate can and will do what he promises.

The basis of that appeal is that Donald Trump is not one of us. And he is not pretending to be. He presents himself smarter and richer than we are and more importantly "much smarter" and "much richer" than all of the candidates of the "political class" that he is running against.

Unlike the other candidates, his overarching position on all the issues can be summed up as:

> *'I'll manage the hell' out of the government, the people in the government and because our economy and our government will be 'managed efficiently' for a 'change,' we'll make better trade*

deals, have more jobs and better health care. This will result in all of our people (you and me), except the bad guys (the rapists, murderers, and gang members) that I deport and don't let back in our country, leading much healthier and happier lives than ever before. In other words, I'll 'make our country great again.'

How will Trump "manage the hell" out of the economy? The government can't be predicted or spelled out in advance as other conventional candidates try to do because, as Trump forthrightly and correctly points out, events on the national stage and the international stage can never be predicted.

However, "The Donald" tells us:

Don't worry about it. Look what I've done—built huge, impressive buildings, made great deals, and enriched myself in the process by outsmarting other people, including world and business leaders far smarter than my political opponents or their donors. Furthermore, I can't be bought so I can make America great again. They can't stop me … you can believe me. That's all I care about.

The visual and audio of this world presented by Donald Trump is seductive, and his support reflected in the polls documents its attraction. Machiavelli recognized that political judgment to be effective must follow principles more ruthless than those acceptable in ordinary life, when he wrote in *The Prince*, "it is necessary for a prince wishing to hold his own to know how to do wrong and to make use of it or not according to necessity."

"Prince Donald" presents his character and his history convincingly as evidence that among the candidates in both parties, he, alone, understands that and will act upon it.

He illustrates his point by applying the different standards of private life and even the business world from which he comes to the political and personal judgments of him by the media and his political opponents.

In private life, you take attacks personally, whereas the conventional wisdom in politics is that if you take attacks or judgments about you personally, you display vulnerability because you "don't understand" that "all politics is theater."

Well, Donald Trump defies the conventional wisdom. He at least pretends to take attacks, judgments, or even questions by his political opponents and the media personally, and he fires back enthusiastically going to "war with vitriolic words" much as we would; and because of this other worldly response, a portion of us loves it or at least enjoys watching and hearing the reality show that follows.

How much longer this will play out remains to be seen. A more important question would be: how would this private and very different world transition into governance if it doesn't go away? This is at least a possibility no longer to be completely discounted.

Trump's world is perhaps even less real than the world of the other politicians he so far has successfully scoffed at rhetorically and otherwise. As Michael Ignatieff, Canadian author, academic, and former politician, has pointed out:

> *Politicians who wish to actually govern cannot cocoon themselves in the inner world of their own imaginings. They must not confuse the world as it is with the world as they wish it to be.*

Experience, including the different experience exhibited so pointedly by Donald Trump, can confine rather than broaden a leader's ability to address events and issues.

NBC political director and *Meet the Press* moderator Chuck Todd presciently tried to address this by asking candidate Trump who would be his advisors on foreign policy, ISIS, etc., if he were to become president of the United States. Donald Trump's answer was not a confidence-builder. He basically responded that he hadn't really thought about it, but for the time being, he got his information from watching the talk shows. So do I. But I'm not running for president of the United States.

Chapter 9

Political Choices Should Be Reality-Based and Checked

*"The danger with any politician is that he or she
will start believing his or her own handlers,
press releases and speeches."*

Michael Ignatieff's ideas on "political judgment should inform our observations, opinions, and perhaps even our decisions about which politician to vote for in Maryland's February 12, 2008, primaries. Michael Ignatieff is a former professor at Harvard University and contributing writer for the *New York Times*, and is now a member of Canada's Parliament and deputy leader of the Liberal Party of Canada.

As February 12, 2008, approaches we have two politicians in the Democratic Party to observe and ultimately choose from when we enter the voting booth, if we are registered Democrats.

One promises "change" and cites his ability to inspire heretofore antagonistic political forces to work together and previously irreconcilable ideas to blend with each other by the force of his calming personality and the "hope" that is the inevitable product of his lofty rhetoric.

The other campaigns on her "experience" and implicitly her ability to actually effect "change," based on "being ready to be president on day one."

The change that each promises is at best undefined, except that both clearly would "pull our combat troops out of Iraq quicker than any Republican and provide adequate health care for greater numbers of our citizens, particularly children."

In the Republican Party, there are also two major candidates. One essentially campaigns on his personality of being honest, traveling in his vehicle, which is both rhetorically and on the ground known as the "Straight Talk Express." He promises honesty, integrity, and a willingness to make tough and perhaps unpopular decisions, including supporting an unpopular war and being honest about it with the people.

His MBA opponent markets his positions based on what he perceives will sell the latest technique, being that he is a "change agent" because he has served as an elected official in Washington, D.C., and because his experience in the private sector will enable him to harness global economic forces and halt economic trends resulting from globalization, which appear irreversible. What he would do and how he would do it remains unclear at best.

These four politicians are all at risk for the same reasons. As a very wise man who was a mentor of mine and a successful manager of politicians and politics, said of him and others on more than one occasion:

> *The danger with any politician is that he or she will start believing his or her own handlers, press releases and speeches.*

This is another way of saying what Michael Ignatieff points out:

> *Politicians cannot afford to cocoon themselves in the inner world of their own imaginings. They must not confuse the world as it is with the world as they wish it to be.*

Once again, I submit that the key to doing that for a politician is putting the right people in the room with him or her and listening to them before making important decisions. These should be wise men and women who will speak the truth to those in power and who are willing to admit their own and the politician's past mistakes, and counsel the leader they are advising to avoid repeating them.

These are people who recognize that the way any of us can improve our grasp of reality is to confront the world without preconception every day and learn mostly from our mistakes what works and what doesn't work, while at the same time recognizing that even lengthy experience can fail us in life and politics.

Again, as Ignatieff points out:

> *Experience can imprison decision makers in worn out solutions while blinding them to the untried remedy that does the trick.*

A sense of reality, however, is not just a sense of the world as it is, but as it might be. Ignatieff writes,

> *Like great artists, great politicians see possibilities others cannot and then seek to turn them into realities.*

To bring the new into being, however, will clearly require more than inspiring rhetoric. If that was all it took, we would be there already. There has been no shortage of speeches, some sending all of our hopes skyward, from Barack Obama and others in this campaign season. Clearly, those speeches have not and will not by themselves take this country where we want it to go as a society.

Ignatieff states:

> *To bring the new into being, a politician needs a sense of timing of when to leap and when to remain still.*

Otto Von Bismarck, the Iron Chancellor of Germany, famously remarked:

> *Political judgment is the ability to hear before anyone else the distant hoof beats of the horse of history.*

Samuel Beckett's "Worstward Ho" (*Fail again, Fail better*) captured an even clearer perspective on the inner obstinacy necessary to the political art. Winston Churchill and Charles de Gaulle kept faith with their own judgment even when elite opinion strongly believed them to be mistaken. Their willingness to wait for historical validation looks like greatness now.

Contrast that view with how you think history will view the current president and those supporters of the way he led us into the War in Iraq and his conduct of that war ever since. Is he a great man awaiting history's vindication or is he a stubborn man who had a charmed life surrounded by "Yes men and women" who can't or won't acknowledge and learn from their mistakes? More important, is he capable of asking himself that question?

In fact, as it turns out in politics, good judgment depends on being a critical judge of one self. People with good judgment listen to warning bells within. Prudent leaders force themselves to listen equally to advocates and opponents of the course of action they are thinking of pursuing. They do not suppose that they know all they need to know, and they do not suppose that good intentions will guarantee good results.

Most importantly, a good leader recognizes his or her own personal limitation from which prudence arises and upon which sound judgment relies. Which one or more of the candidates understands themselves well enough to exercise sound judgment and be an effective leader?

Ask yourself that question when you decide whom to vote for on February 12, 2008. How will that candidate govern if elected? Stay for that discussion.

Chapter 10

Politics as Theater

*"Nothing is personal in politics
because politics is theater."*

"How will they govern if elected?" That was the question with which I ended my column published on February 8, 2008. Since that date, the "they" has been reduced by one. Mitt Romney has withdrawn. So Senator John McCain, Senator Hillary Rodham Clinton, or Senator Barack Obama will be the next president of the United States.

Which one of these candidates is the most likely to effectively exercise political power and discretion?

Michael Ignatieff, former Harvard University professor, contributing writer for the *New York Times*, a current member of Canada's Parliament and deputy leader of Canada's Liberal Party, assesses the overall probability that any of these candidates will do that as, at best, unlikely. In doing so, he recounts a British prime minister's comment when asked what made his job so difficult. "Events, dear boy," the prime minister instantly replied.

"Few of us hear the horses coming," says Ignatieff. The few that do recognize, as did Niccolò Machiavelli, that political judgment to be effective must follow principles more ruthless than those acceptable in ordinary life.

As Ignatieff points out, Franklin D. Roosevelt and Winston Churchill knew how to do wrong, yet they did not demand to be judged by different ethical standards than their fellow citizens did. They accepted that democratic leaders cannot make up their own moral rules, and these strictures apply both at home and abroad.

If President George W. Bush and his "team" had "heard the horses coming" and not demanded to be judged by different legal and ethical standards than their fellow citizens of the United States and the world, then would there have been the issues raised over Guantanamo and Abu Ghraib or anywhere else? The answer is probably not!

In some areas, however, political and personal judgments are very different. Ignatieff illustrates several of these areas. In private life, you take attacks personally. You would be considered cold and unfeeling if you didn't. In politics, the conventional wisdom is that if you take attacks personally, you display vulnerability. Politicians, therefore, try to appear invulnerable without appearing inhuman.

The conventional wisdom in politics is as Ignatieff points out, "Nothing is personal in politics because politics is theater." This is exhibited over and over again in legislatures where legislators insult one another in the chamber and then retreat for a drink at a bar or a restaurant afterward. This institutionalized hypocrisy is generally not available in private life. There, we mean what we say, say what we mean, and we plan revenge for being insulted.

We do, however, in private life put less emphasis on words than on what we mean by them. There is no such courtesy in politics. In public life, language is a weapon of war and is deployed in a way that engenders radical distrust of politicians. All that matters is what you said not what you meant. Everything said in politics is potentially open to be taken literally.

Examples are Senator John McCain's comment about "being in Iraq for a hundred years"; President Bill Clinton's comment about Barack Obama's politics on Iraq being a "fantasy" and his acknowledgment of Ronald Reagan's transformative presidency; Hillary Clinton's "racially insensitive" comment about the relationship between Rev. Dr. Martin Luther King, Jr. and President Lyndon Johnson's accomplishments in the field of civil rights.

There is starting to be an adverse reaction to "politics as theater." This reaction has been noticed and is being monitored and even pandered to by all three presidential campaigns in the form of their scripted message of "change."

This "change" is defined differently by each candidate because they are appealing to different constituencies. The change desired by those constituencies is different and in some respects conflicted.

Politics is still theater in 2008. Campaigns are the warm-up for the final Act of Governance. As we are all learning, campaigns do not help us measure a candidate's ability to exercise good judgment. Campaigns and primaries test a candidate's charm, stamina, money-raising ability, and rhetorical powers but not their leadership skills, judgment, and coolness under fire.

Chapter 11

President of the United States: A Job Description

*"CEO needed to supervise 2.6 million employees ...
willing to work at home ...
spectacular public failure likely."*

How would the remaining candidates for president of the United States govern if elected? This is the threshold and clearly the most important question we should answer before we decide who should be the next "Leader of The Free World."

Our first, and in my view, the paramount inquiry in answering that question is who would be in the room when important decisions are made, particularly those related to foreign policy/national security, economic policy, and judicial appointments (ok, my personal interest and bias are showing).

As *Washington Post* national reporter Joel Achenbach recently pointed out in his blog and in the Outlook Section of the *Washington Post*, if you had to craft a help wanted advertisement for the position of "President of The United States," you would write something like:

CEO needed to supervise 2.6 million employees. Must be at least 35, native-born, and willing to work at home. Spectacular public failure likely.

President Franklin D. Roosevelt in 1937 wrote:

The President's task has become impossible for me or any other man ... a man in this position will not be able to survive White House Service unless it is simplified. I need executive assistants with a 'passion for anonymity' to be my legs.

In response to this presidential self-assessment, a report by a committee headed by Louis Brownlow, an expert in public administration, concluded that "a half-dozen senior advisors would make the White House a more effective operation."

Acting on that recommendation, Congress in 1939 created the Executive Office of The President (EOP). Today, the "half-dozen senior advisors" has grown to about 3,000 staffers. That does not include, Achenbach reports, the 15 departments run by cabinet secretaries or any of the other agencies that are part of the Executive Branch.

This documents the premise first articulated by Richard Neustadt in his seminal text, *Presidential Power and Modern Presidents*:

No president can spread himself across the whole of the post-Roosevelt government.

The modern solution to this dilemma by Roosevelt and his successors has been to expand the number of the president's "Executive Assistants" "to act as his legs" in almost centipede-like fashion throughout the bureaucracy. This most dramatically includes the president's personal and political staff and his staff's assistants in the White House.

This trend coupled with adapting and experimenting with various methods and models of executive decision-making has produced as many failures as successes.

Joel Achenbach points out, as has this writer, the literature in presidential decision-making repeatedly returns to a central premise:

A president needs to be good at making decisions, lots of them on complicated matters.

I would add that he or she needs to be able to do that systematically and once done not agonize or temporize. At the same time, the president should be willing to reconsider a decision when subsequent experience makes it clear that it was a bad decision and needs to be corrected.

That means that the president must talk to different people about different things. He or she must also talk to more than one set of advisors about the same thing. The structure of how the president receives this advice should be designed in a way that ensures that even if the president is naturally conflict-averse, as most successful politicians are, that all ideas are timely considered fully and completely in a framework and atmosphere in which the leader is not unduly pressured in a particular direction based solely on who is in the room when the decision is reached.

Furthermore, the system should not depend on the president "begging for bad news"—which again considering the prevalent "conflict-averse" personality of the people who are elected political leaders as well as the desire by many of them to be liked or even loved—is not likely to happen.

As Joel Achenbach notes:

The last century is littered with failed or mediocre presidencies. The job crushed men who once strode the landscape like titans. They self-destructed in some cases or had no business being in the job in the first place.

Achenbach makes these statements but doesn't reference particular presidents when doing so, leaving his readers and mine to fill in the blanks. The only specific president he mentions is the incumbent who is referenced with the comment:

> *A number of historians have asserted that he is the worst Presi-*
> *dent the Nation has ever had, which if nothing else, is the best*
> *news that fans of Warren G. Harding have had in years.*

So, who can we expect to be in the Oval Office advising a President Barack Obama, a President Hillary Rodham Clinton, or a President John McCain, and what is the universe of ideas they will bring to the hopefully large and diversely populated hyperbolic conference table next to The Oval Office?

Equally important, what method or model of decision-making would ensure the highest quality of presidential decision-making?

Clearly, we don't know. Campaigns don't inform voters on these subjects. As Robert Caro, two-time Pulitzer Prize–winning biographer of Lyndon Johnson, has pointed out about presidential campaigns:

> *There's endless months of debating about this job and almost*
> *no public discussion of what the job is.*

Caro illustrates his point by citing examples: (1) Lyndon Johnson wound up poring over bombing charts from Vietnam; (2) Jimmy Carter was so detail-obsessed that he reportedly approved requests to use the White House tennis court; according to Professor Roger Porter, who teaches about "The American Presidency at Harvard," Carter got enmeshed in parking assignments at the Department of the Interior as well as the "crucial issue" of "federal cotton-dust standards."

Who, among us, who have worked with CEOs in all branches of government at every level and even with medium-to-large bureaucracies in both the public and private sectors, have not observed—if not directly experienced ourselves—leaders who preoccupy themselves with minutiae in lieu of making important policy and personal decisions as a means of avoiding the stress that accompanies making the more important decisions?

What is clear then is that the job of president of the United States requires, as Robert Caro says, "an enormously flexible mind." I would add to that the essential discipline and ability to compartmentalize and, in doing so, to rationally prioritize decisions in very different areas and on very different issues on the basis of their importance and time sensitiveness as opposed to what issue was presented first and what would be the most fun. This is necessary while maintaining broad intellectual curiosity.

There are more solid hints as to each of the remaining candidates' decision-making styles and discipline, as well as the identity of their circle of advisors and the extent of their intellectual curiosity and interest in the areas of foreign policy/national security, economic policy, and judicial appointments, respectively.

Chapter 12

The Political Art of Holding Your Tongue and Thinking Your Piece

*"The rule of thumb is never tell the President
what he doesn't want to hear."*

Who would be in the room when important decisions are made by a President John McCain, a President Barack Obama, or a President Hillary Rodham Clinton? We, of course, don't know.

What we do know is that the president's decision-making style will significantly drive his or her initial selection of advisors and, equally important, which advisors stay in any administration. The president of the United States, or for that matter any chief executive at any level of government or private enterprise, needs as many counselors and advisors as possible who are not so employed or occupied because they need the job economically or psychologically, *i.e.*, there is a market and a job for them and their skill-sets outside the Executive's Office.

In other words, they could find alternative employment in places where they would enjoy their work, use their skills, be professionally and personally fulfilled, as well as support themselves and their families.

Implementation of this "qualification" for at least some advisors and counselors to the executive at every level of government would make it more likely that the president, governor, or even local or private executive would have advisors of substance and stature, who would speak the truth to power when it is called for without fear of losing the only job in the world that can provide them with professional recognition and fulfillment as well as economic sustenance to support themselves and their families.

The fact that an executive would bring such a person into his or her administration would itself be encouraging particularly if he or she did it knowingly and intentionally; it would mean that the executive is not so insecure or conflict-averse that he or she can't tolerate even private disagreement or other "bad news." In turn, this would at least make it more likely, if not ensure, that executive decisions would be reality-based.

History is replete with examples of what happens when the contrary is true. Some of these examples and the people in them are surprising. Michael Powell reports on what he describes as the "heartache" of White House Staff in 1966 "caught between apprehension of looming disaster in Vietnam and the need for candor with their boss, President Lyndon Baines Johnson."

To these aides, says Powell, "Disaster seemed a safer choice." Powell cites historian Arthur Schlesinger Jr.'s account of then–Defense Secretary Robert McNamara's selection as the "most logical candidate to speak the truth to his boss" since he had told Schlesinger and economist John Kenneth Galbraith that he regarded "a military solution as impossible."

Notwithstanding his position, several months later, McNamara was still publicly urging a widening of the war.

Schlesinger then reports that advisors turned to Ambassador W. Averill Harriman to say and do what needed to be done. It was not to be. Alas, Schlesinger noted in his *Journals: 1952–2000* of his friend, Harriman:

Everyone has his weaknesses, and Averill's is the desire to be near power.

Next, out of desperation and frustration, reality-based advisors who cared about the country and the president turned to Vice President Hubert H. Humphrey, soon-to-be presidential candidate, whom Schlesinger reports offered only "unctuous smiles."

Humphrey's trouble, as analyzed by Schlesinger, was "that he could not say something publicly without deeply believing it privately; and when as now, he has no choice in his public utterances, he whips up a fervency of private belief."

Schlesinger draws some historical lessons from this and other illustrative historical events. His conclusion is:

To be a White House Adviser is to occupy a peculiarly circumscribed world. You can be a confidant to the most powerful leader in the world, you can fetch his coffee or write brilliant briefs on nuclear disarmament, ride in limousines, share the corner office and chuckle over martinis with the wife of the French Ambassador (times have changed since Schlesinger wrote this. If you chuckle over martinis with the wife of the French Ambassador, you will probably read about it and then be summarily shown the door)! *But the coin of your realm is your relationship to one man. Displease him and your wilderness beckons.*

Another historian, Richard Reeves, further reinforces this historical assessment when he concludes:

The rule of thumb is never tell the President what he doesn't want to hear.

David Halberstam weighs in as well by illustration when he points out that there was one similarity between Mao Zedong and Douglas MacArthur:

Neither of their staffs ever told them a thing they didn't want to hear.

Nevertheless, our best presidents have broken this historical model, which tells this writer, to borrow from President Barack Obama's phrase, "the audacity to hope," that the next president will do likewise.

Charles B. Strozier, a history professor at John Jay College of Criminal Justice and author of *Lincoln's Quest for Union: A Psychological Portrait*, reports that Lincoln was "comfortable with the discord" among cabinet and staff, which was "filled with contentious personalities, several of whom considered themselves superior to the President." Yet, it bore little resemblance to the modern institution.

Notwithstanding his selection and retention of these "strong personalities," Strozier reports that "Lincoln absolutely had control of his cabinet, but not in a way that prevented him from hearing dissenting views."

Doris Kearns Goodwin, another historian and presidential scholar, cites yet another of our best presidents, Franklin D. Roosevelt, pointing out that although he "inspired intense loyalty," he was psychologically secure and politically confident enough to invite prominent Republicans into his cabinet as World War II loomed in 1941.

"Roosevelt was forgiving of disagreement," according to David M. Kennedy, a Stanford University historian. "But once a decision was made it was incumbent to shut up or get out," writes Kennedy. In other words, Roosevelt admired and even enforced what Arthur Schlesinger, Jr. described as "the political art of holding your tongue while thinking your piece."

John F. Kennedy encouraged and enforced this political art and skill most illustratively in the "Cuban Missile Crisis" when he listened to the Joint Chiefs of Staff, whom Schlesinger reports "barely blanched at the prospect of a nuclear war." But he instead decided to negotiate and, in doing so, step back from the breach.

President Kennedy, as written by his friend, John Kenneth Galbraith, in his book, *Name Dropping*, made it very clear that "no one could fail his test of loyalty." When Chester Bowles, an advisor, did so by speaking out about his opposition to the Bay of Pigs Invasion after the fact, apparently mistaking President Kennedy's willingness to listen for a willingness to have his policy questioned publicly, Bowles found out that the penalty for failing the loyalty test was quick and direct.

President Kennedy crafted an "ingenious gallows." Bowles was promoted to "non-employment in the White House—to no function and a general requirement of silence," reports Galbraith. Bowles, who Galbraith characterizes as "the man who almost certainly would have been the chief critic of the emerging Vietnam disaster, was safely contained."

But was that in the interest of the president or the country? As to the first part of the question, debatable; as to the second part, clearly not.

Which one or more of the current presidential candidates is most likely to encourage "the political art of holding your tongue while thinking your piece," and who are the best and brightest practitioners of the "Art" on the scene for them to include in the administration?

Chapter 13

Political Judgment Is Not Science – It's About People

"What is called wisdom in statesmen is understanding, rather than knowledge ..."

My last column, which began the New Year, was aptly titled "Let Us Resolve to Find the Best Leaders in Every Field." With that resolution and the four columns that preceded it headlined "Facing the Challenge of Finding and Picking Good Judges," I found myself continuing to reflect on an article written by Michael Ignatieff, a former professor at Harvard University and contributing writer for the *New York Times*, who is now a member of Canada's Parliament and deputy leader of the Liberal Party of Canada.

That article, which appeared in the August 5, 2007, *New York Times* magazine was entitled, "Getting Iraq Wrong: What the War Has Taught Me about Political Judgment." Its significance is not its commentary on the narrow topic of what went wrong in the decision-making of not only the president of the United States, but also of the writers, pundits, and academic commentators who supported the invasion of Iraq, among whom the author includes himself.

Rather, what is important here is Ignatieff's analysis of the difference between what constitutes "good judgment" in politics and what "good judgment" is and looks like in intellectual life. The most poignant as well as the most durable ideas, which he presents in this discussion, should inform our observations and the opinions we form about everything from watching presidential debates to selecting our leaders in all three branches of government at the federal, state, and local levels.

As Ignatieff points out, referencing the work of philosopher Isaiah Berlin, whom this writer has written about previously admiring his most famous essay, "The Hedge Hog and The Fox," in a column published last June 25, 2007, the attribute that underpins "good judgment" in politicians is a sense of reality, which is to be distinguished from what is considered "good judgment in intellectual life."

Among intellectuals, judgment is about generalizing and interpreting particular facts as instances of some big idea. In politics, specifics matter more than generalities. Theory can often get in the way of a politician's understanding what the true reality is.

Isaiah Berlin clarifies this by writing with reference to figures like Franklin D. Roosevelt and Winston Churchill saying:

> *What is called wisdom in statesmen is understanding, rather than knowledge—some kind of acquaintance with relevant facts of such a kind that enable those who have it to tell what fits with what; what can be done in given circumstances and what cannot, what means will work in what situations and how far, without necessarily being able to explain how they know this or even what they know."*

This means that politicians can't confuse the world as it is with the world as they wish it to be.

This very much comports with my belief, reinforced as I get older and more observant, that the most important factor affecting the quality of political decision-making is who is in the room and who is heard before the decision is made.

In practical politics, as Michael Ignatieff points out:

> *There is no science of decision-making—the vital judgments a politician makes every day are about people: whom to trust, whom to believe and whom to avoid.*

Having good judgment in these matters and having a sound sense of reality requires trusting some very unscientific instincts and intuitions about people.

This contrasts with the world occupied by academics and commentators. As Berlin once pointed out, they care more about whether ideas are interesting than whether they are true.

Politicians live by ideas just as much as professional thinkers do, but they don't have the time or the patience to consider ideas that are merely interesting. They have to confine their attention to the small number of ideas that have the virtue of being true and the even smaller number that actually apply to real life.

In academic and intellectual life, false ideas can still be fun to play with. In political life, false ideas can ruin the lives of millions and useless ones can waste precious human and fiscal resources.

An intellectual's responsibility is to master the consequences of his ideas wherever they may lead.

A politician's responsibility is to master these consequences and prevent from doing harm.

How does this apply to the issues facing our country and our state?

Chapter 14

Political Theater Need Not Be Children's Theater

"The time has come to set aside childish things."

As different worlds collide in our state and country, indeed in the world, I keep thinking of what I consider the most important idea expressed by President Barack Obama in his 2008 Inaugural Address and the words he used to express it:

The time has come to set aside childish things.

The childish things or habits that we ought to set aside are displayed on the stage of the "political theater" that our elected and appointed leaders regularly present to us to gain acceptance of or at least acquiescence to politically controversial decisions.

Those decisions and the policies embodied in them emerge after original legislative, executive, and regulatory ideas are scrutinized and modified by compromise as a result of being subjected to what my more elitist friends and writers describe as "the messy workings of the political marketplace." The political marketplace of our constitutional representative democracy is a colorful collage of interest groups, large and small, governmental and non-governmental, economic, corporate, environmental, sectarian and non-sectarian.

As Nicholas Leman, a critic-at-large for *The New Yorker* magazine, who has analyzed Arthur Fisher Bentley's *The Process of Government: A Study of Social Pressures*, points out:

> *For Bentley, every political force that matters is an interest group, regardless of whether it cops to the charge or not, States and cities are 'locality groups,' income categories are 'wealth groups,' devoted followers of a popular politician or a cause are 'personality groups.'*

Under Bentley's theory, when groups are comprehensively and accurately depicted and assembled on the stage of our political theater, "everything is stated and accounted for."

If Bentley's theory is accepted, you can't talk about collective "public opinion" because there is no such thing as "the public" (there are only diverse groups). Likewise, terms such as "the public interest" and "the popular will" bandied about by politicians seeking approval or even affection from "the people" have no real substantive content because "there is nothing which is best literally for the whole people."

Bentley's construct of reality is more clearly understood by realizing that he generally divides interest groups into two categories: (1) Organization Groups (*e.g.*, The American Association of Retired Persons (AARP), The National Association of Broadcasters, Chambers of Commerce, and AFL-CIO) and (2) "Talk Groups," which encompass all those who "claim" to represent "the public interest" or a "good cause," *e.g.*, journalists, reformers, think tanks, humanitarians, and policy analysts.

The influence of "Talk Groups" is, in Bentley's view, "vastly overestimated and overvalued." In fact, as Nicholas Leman points out, Bentley goes further than most, including this writer, in labeling "anyone who comes into public life claiming *not* to have an interest as either deluded or deceitful."

Now "political theater" is not necessarily "children's theater." But sometimes the political actors and actresses who produce it seem to think it has to be in order for their decisions to be accepted.

The politicians, their staffs, consultants, pollsters, and policymakers accept the conventional wisdom of their "elite" class that "the people" want politics to have good guys and bad guys, good policies and bad policies, etc. In other words, they presume that "we" want politics in our intentionally designed complex system of constitutionally-based checks and balances to be simple even if it is not.

They want us to ignore the reality that people get involved in politics to get what they want, which may or may not entail economic advantage, power, prestige, or influence for themselves, their organizations, or their causes.

Finally, nobody is a member of only one interest group, and no interest group stands apart from other groups and behaves in a single consistent and totally rational way that elevates them above the rest or legitimizes any claim they may make to be "the true voice of the people."

The result, as Bentley describes it, is reality. Intelligent actions, emotional actions, linked actions, trains of action, planned actions, plotted actions, scheming, experimenting, persisting, exhorting, compelling, mastering, struggling, cooperating—such activities by the thousands we find going on around us in populations among which we are placed.

Accepting that this is the result of the democracy that our "Founders," who themselves represented various interest groups, created is to accept reality. To do so is neither cynical nor depressing. As it did when Bentley helped organize progressive Robert La Follette's presidential campaign in 1924, it can serve as a "Call to Action."

That is, in fact, exactly what the Obama administration is saying and doing when its rhetoric suggests that it will "change the old way of doing things" and "clean up the mess in Washington." That is also clearly what the administration is doing now when it plans to "mobilize its internet network of supporters" in support of the legislation to adopt the president's budget and priorities.

Applying Bentley's analytical framework, the administration is simply adjusting the correlation of and balance of forces among interest groups, bringing some into power and relegating others who were elevated for the last eight years to lesser positions.

Hopefully, both those who are being "elevated to greater positions of power" as well as those "relegated to lesser positions" by the new administration will have, or develop, the analytical skills to recognize that this is the natural ebb and flow of the workings of our democracy and not the result of either the "promptings of pure justice" or "the corruption of the system" by the political opponents of the previous administration and its supporters.

If they do, then civility will govern relations inside and outside all three branches of government, motives will not be questioned without evidence of wrongdoing, bipartisanship will occasionally be possible and when it isn't, issues will be resolved as a result of politicians, agencies, and courts working through the political and economic issues that are too mundane to be a part of the public conversation but are nevertheless important.

"And, yes, Virginia," this will be accomplished with the help of lawyers and "heaven forbid" lobbyists.

PART TWO

Advanced Governing

Chapter 15

The Act of Governance – What Matters

*"Politicians with good judgment bend the policy
to fit the human timber."*

The Republican presidential primary season, while still ongoing, is practically over. Senator John McCain barring an unprecedented faux pas, will be the Republican Party's nominee for president and he's already playing the role by rhetorically attacking the man he believes he will be running against in the fall general election campaign, Senator Barack Obama.

Senator Hillary Clinton and Senator Obama are more cautious for sound political and personal reasons. They continue to campaign against each other, in the case of Clinton, furiously, in what increasingly looks like a last ditch effort with every political weapon at hand to change the "campaign's narrative" and the theme from "The Barack Obama Phenomenon/Movement/Momentum" to one she and her husband remember affectionately and would like to embrace completely one more time, "The Comeback Kid."

That role, for mathematical reasons, may escape her; even if she wins the next few primaries, because of the Democratic Party's rules, which award delegates proportionately, it will be difficult for her to catch up even with more "wins" than "losses" in the remaining state contests. That political reality has obviously not persuaded Senator Clinton and her campaign's managers and advisors that the fight is not worth continuing.

The most recent weapon that they have unveiled is a television advertisement aired in all of the media markets where the campaign is raging. It depicts a young, female child peacefully sleeping in her bed in a typical suburban middle-class home in a typical middle-class subdivision, when at 3:00 am, unbeknownst to her, the red telephone in the White House rings, presumably with news of some international crisis or emergency that is not defined or even described.

The voice in the ad then rhetorically asks who the viewer/voter would want to answer the telephone. The Clinton campaign clearly thinks the voters viewing the ad will somehow be persuaded by this visual to answer, Senator Clinton, because of the experience and history she brings to the task.

The Obama campaign responded within record time, thereby giving new dimension to the term "Rapid Reply," with a television ad that repeated the visual but pointed out that when the closest thing to such a call was in fact received by Clinton, she arguably did the "wrong thing" by voting to give President Bush the authority to invade Iraq while Senator Obama opposed it.

Both these ads serve as metaphors for addressing the issue of how these candidates will govern if elected. They also continue to illustrate, as I have emphasized, that politics is theater and that campaigns, including ads such as these, are not particularly helpful in measuring a candidate's ability to exercise good judgment and govern effectively.

The reality is that neither Senator Clinton nor Senator Obama, or for that matter Senator McCain, have any life experience that illustrates their ability to govern effectively in this type of "crisis"; nor does anyone else who has not already occupied the Office of President of the United States.

Simply living in the White House, whether as first lady or otherwise, even if while you were there you observed your spouse, who was the president of the United States, receive and respond to these types of calls, does not necessarily or logically translate into the ability to effectively respond to and manage such emergency calls or other situations.

Likewise, Senator Obama's stated opposition to the war in Iraq, even to his most partisan supporters, cannot be logically put forward as evidence of his ability to effectively govern an unanticipated crisis.

That reality also encompasses the life history, admirable experience, and heroic story that Senator McCain would bring to the Oval Office. Having been a prisoner of war, soldier, courageous political warrior, etc., does not provide evidence of competence to act in a worldwide political, diplomatic crisis or even military emergency.

What does provide such evidence or at least hint at what matters? Here, if we as readers, listeners, and voters take the step toward being willing to believe these candidates when they talk about how they would approach the job of governance, their words may actually be illuminating.

Again, the analysis offered by Michael Ignatieff, former Harvard University professor, contributing writer for the *New York Times*, now deputy leader of Canada's Liberal Party and a member of Canadian Parliament, is probative. Ignatieff, in discussing the importance of the tension and ultimately the balance that should be struck between "principles" and "compromise," says, "Good judgment means understanding how to be responsible to those who pay the price of your decisions."

To illustrate his point, Ignatieff cites the historical instance when the British political philosopher, Edmund Burke, when first elected to The House of Commons, told the voters of Bristol who had elected him that "he would never sacrifice his judgment to the pressure of their opinion."

Ignatieff takes issue with Burke's position. So does this writer. As Ignatieff, himself a Canadian legislator and party leader, points out:

> *Sometimes sacrificing my judgment to theirs is the essence of my job, provided, of course, that I don't sacrifice my principles.*

Ignatieff explains further:

> *Fixed principle matters. There are some goods that cannot be traded, some lines that cannot be crossed, some people who must never be betrayed, but fixed ideas of a dogmatic kind are usually the enemy of good judgment.*

To illustrate this point, Ignatieff opines as an example:

> *It is an obstacle to clear thinking to believe that America's foreign policy serves God's plan to expand human freedom. Ideological thinking of this sort bends what Kant called 'The crooked timber of humanity' to fit an abstract illusion. Politicians with good judgment bend the policy to fit the human timber. Not all good things, after all, can be had together, whether in life or in politics.*

Isn't this demonstrably true? In fact, in the real world, bad public policy can and often does turn out to be very popular in short-term politics, does it not? Simply because resisting the popular will isn't easy does not mean that it is the right thing to do or that it is wise to do so.

As Ignatieff observes:

> *Good judgment in politics is messy. It means balancing policy and politics in imperfect compromises that always leave someone unhappy—often yourself.*

In a representative democracy such as ours, Ignatieff notes that:

> *[K]owing the difference between a good and a bad compromise is more important than holding to pure principle at any price. A good compromise restores the peace and enables parties to go about their business with some element of their vital interest*

satisfied. A bad one surrenders the public interest to compul-
sion of force.

With this in mind, what words or message from Senator Clinton, Senator Obama, and Senator McCain should we be paying attention to? Read on next time to answer that question.

Chapter 16

How Will Candidates Govern? The Most Important Question Not Easily Answered

"You can't govern by polls, but you need the American people with you to govern effectively."

What are the differences in how the three candidates, who have survived their respective political parties' nominating processes to this date, would govern? That question is not as easily answered as we would think or even hope despite our observing over two years of campaigning by all of them.

Campaigns and primaries test a candidate's charm, stamina, money-raising ability, and rhetorical powers, but not their leadership skills, judgment, and coolness under fire.

Attempts to draw conclusions about what any of the candidate's governing style and substance would be from their handling of the day-to-day events and issues that arise on the campaign trail would inevitably fail the judicial "strict scrutiny test" or even the less rigorous "reasonable relation test."

For example, Senator Barack Obama's rhetorical handling of the controversy generated by some of his Pastor Jeremiah Wright's sermons for the last 20 years didn't tell us very much about how Obama would govern if he is elected president of the United States.

This is true regardless of whether you think Obama's speech was "magnificent"—"an extremely important step forward in this country's effort to transcend its racial history and divisions"—or whether you believe it was essentially a politically fine-tuned statement designed to mitigate the damage that the media's sustained focus on Reverend Wright's arguably incendiary and to some voters offensive rhetoric, and Senator Obama's concurrent 20-year personal and spiritual relationship with him while he was using these "fighting words" or "inspirational words."

What you think will obviously depend on your historical perspective and perhaps your racial and ethnic background and age.

What it does is focus our attention on the indisputable fact that we humans, including politicians, are all more complicated than either our admirers or detractors want to admit, and that the "inconvenient truth" sometimes gets in the way of staying on message as well as acknowledging reality in the day-to-day rough and tumble of a political campaign.

The truth here is that all of the descriptions of Senator Obama's speech as well as his actions over his adult lifetime were and are like most of us, including Reverend Wright, motivated by a variety of historical, biological, psychological, and environmental forces as well as circumstance. It is not late-breaking news that some of these factors and circumstances can be controlled and some cannot.

Likewise, Senator Hillary Clinton's recent gaffes describing her landing in Bosnia in terms more violent, colorful, and dramatic than it was, as well as her obstinacy in remaining in the race for president, do not tell us much about how she would govern in style or substance as president of the United States.

There are obviously those in the opposition camps who would like to draw profound conclusions from what they view as "bizarre behavior" in the first instance and in the second instance "selfishness," *i.e.,* caring more about her personal ambition than the Party. But her explanation for the first event, which was "inaccurate memory" and "lack of sleep," ought to be given credence in the absence of clinical evidence that would cast doubt upon it.

With respect to her determination to remain in the race until all the primary voters have spoken (including Florida and Michigan), even Senator Obama concedes that it is her right and not inappropriate under the rules and the deadlines established by the Democratic National Committee.

Furthermore, it is noteworthy that Senator Obama is not among those verbally attempting "to pressure her out," although he does not appear to have persuaded his own campaign staff and surrogates to follow his lead. He would be wise to do so if his campaign's basic message that his "Words Do Matter" is not to be downsized in the face of conflicting and confusing messages from his staff and surrogates. These messages were recently characterized by *New York Times* op/ed. columnist Maureen Dowd, exaggerating and paraphrasing from the famous scene of the *Wizard of Oz* in which the wicked witch warns the heroin, "Surrender Already, Dorothy."

Senator John McCain may well present the most interesting as well as the most difficult campaign to try to analyze how he would govern in style and substance. This difficulty is despite of, or perhaps because of, his comparatively much longer career in public service. That career, however, has been as a soldier and as a legislator in Congress, and as a now two-time presidential candidate. That history demonstrates some relevant personality traits from which both positive and negative inferences can rationally be drawn about how he would govern.

My problem is, as I observe him, every time I think I can draw conclusions about how he would govern, he announces a position that contradicts or at least muddles my previous impression.

I recognize that Senator McCain is doing this now because he has the luxury of having wrapped up the Republican Party nomination and can use this time (which the Democrats are giving him) to "reintroduce" himself to the nation's voters, notwithstanding his long history and exposure to them.

I also understand that while we observe his "reintroduction," he is clearly moving to the political center and away from George W. Bush, which is necessary for him to be competitive in the general election. This accounts for much of the difficulty in predicting how he would govern.

A recent book by Lou Cannon and Carl M. Cannon, father and son journalists, entitled, *Reagan's Disciple–George W. Bush's Troubled Quest for a Presidential Legacy*, illustrates how difficult it is to discern how a politician will govern or even how he has governed from his campaign rhetoric and public history. As Dick Polman, national political columnist at the *Philadelphia Inquirer*, points out in reviewing the Cannons' book, "Reagan the pragmatic man does not square with Reagan the ideologically conservative myth."

To illustrate their point, the Cannons cite "persuasive evidence to arrive at 'judicious findings' based on the weight of this evidence" that "Reagan wouldn't have gone into Iraq." Reagan "realized that he did not have (nor did he seek) a free hand in waging war." He was "cautious about such involvements" and "believed that modern wars could not be successfully fought without popular domestic support, the requisite troop strength, and a feasible exit strategy." "He was a reluctant warrior who much preferred negotiation to counting the dead."

The Cannons also write that Reagan "was also far more schooled than Bush in the art of compromise and the careful expenditure of political capital." To illustrate this point, they contrast Reagan's "deal" with Tip O'Neill and congressional Democrats in 1983 to keep the Social Security program solvent with Bush's exhausting much of his political capital in 2005 stumping in vain for Social Security privatization—a concept that grew more unpopular the more he talked about it.

Neither of these positions (on the war and the privatization of Social Security) by Bush is a surprise to the Cannons, in light of Bush's and lately his vice president's loud pronouncements that he "pays no attention to polls." However, the Cannons note that notwithstanding his position and image as the "icon of modern conservatism, ... that is not how Reagan governed." Reagan was "guided by his foundational convictions—lower taxes, strong defense, but was attuned to public sentiment and recalibrated when necessary."

As Reagan's last chief of staff, Kenneth Duberstein, told Carl Cannon:

> *You can't govern by polls, but you need the American people with you to govern effectively.*

In addition, the Cannons note that Reagan employed "a diverse and sometimes quarrelsome circle of advisors—people like Duberstein, Howard Baker, George Shultz, and Colin Powell, high-caliber people, who were practical and realistic." This is contrasted with Bush's inner circle, which has never been known for its wide range of opinion nor encouraged to express it. In fact, Reagan in the words of Harvard Professor Joseph Nye, "listened to people who were telling him what was wrong."

George W. Bush, as the Cannons note, has been less tolerant of dissent and more significantly to the detriment of his legacy has "refused to learn from his mistakes."

What does this portend for predicting the governance style and substance of Senators John McCain, Hillary Rodham Clinton, and Barack Obama? What lessons are to be learned from the similar governing styles of Franklin D. Roosevelt and Ronald Reagan, whose philosophical legacies are bipolar but whose style and success were described by Obama as "transformative?"

I'll continue to try based on the limited information revealed by the candidates to answer those questions.

Chapter 17

How Do We Spot Leaders?

*"Commitment is not fashionable: cool is the
order of the day ..."*

How do we spot leaders who are prepared to commit themselves to principles that transcend, but do not necessarily conflict with their personal and political interests, and then elect them? Quoting Daniel Patrick Moynihan, a Democrat with a PhD, who worked as staff for Republican President Richard Nixon, and who was also a professor ambassador and, ultimately, a U.S. senator, who suggested that we would all be better off if we recognized that, in the formulation of public policy:

> We're all entitled to our own opinions, but we're not entitled to
> our own facts.

Well, here is my opinion, in an abbreviated form, on what qualities to look for when choosing Maryland's leaders in the next election. I remind readers that you will be choosing Maryland's legislative and executive branch elected officials for the next four years. They, in turn, will choose their institutional leaders and, within the next few years, a near majority of the unelected judiciary. So we need to be careful, perhaps more careful than we have been in the past, in selecting our elected officials in the next election.

Leadership has been defined in many ways. The one I like best is by a political theorist named Warren Benis:

> *[T]he ability to translate ideas into reality and sustain them over time. That ability encompasses a vision for the future, commitment and perhaps most importantly a willingness to persist.*

Rapid technological change is upon us. The central and most difficult challenge to us as leaders of today is to shape the changing human organization so as to harness these forces in a way that serves all of the people, and to persuade those whose relationship to their company, community, or government is altered by these rapidly emerging technological developments that change is rational and in their interest in the long run.

John F. Kennedy used to talk about leadership quite often. When he did, he used to facetiously quote a long-since forgotten leader of the French Revolution as an anti-role model who said:

> *There go my people. I must find out where they are going so I can lead them.*

I suspect that this individual was and should be forgotten because he thought and said things like that.

To exercise leadership in the new millennium, those we elect and appoint to do so must recognize that our society is so intricately organized that the working of the whole system may be halted if one part stops functioning. Thus, our capacity to frustrate one another through non-cooperation has never been greater. We must, therefore, resolve not to hold the system hostage to anyone's rigid ideological position or institutional intransigence.

This is particularly important in a representative democracy, such as ours, where our elected leaders must balance the need to at least appear to respond to their core constituencies with the need to maintain a vision beyond their constituents' perceived prejudices.

That is not the same, in the words of the forgotten leader of the French Revolution, as "find out where they are going so I can lead them."

Many times, when decisions are made on the great issues of public policy, they are made by leaders balancing the political factors that must be considered—including the feelings of uncertainty, sense of loss, and other stresses that those affected almost always feel in the face of change—with the need to institute change as comprehensively and as rapidly as possible.

What emerges from this process is very often a compromise between the status quo and the comprehensive change sought by its advocates. This degree of change is usually not all of what the proponents of change had sought, but it almost always produces a policy or institution that is better than the idea or organization it replaced. It is also very significantly reconcilable with existing values and needs.

At that point, as leaders, we have a duty to use our abilities—as well as the skills we have developed—to gain acceptance of the compromise to the same extent that we used them to take the lead in the introduction of the new order of things, at least to the extent that stability is restored sufficiently to those affected by the change so that they willingly alter their established relationships in the social organizations and structures in which they live and work.

It does no good to elect men and women of vision and courage to public office and then insist that they take action, albeit innovative and desirable, which will result in their being irreparably damaged or, worse, destroyed politically. Leaders willing to take grave political risks are rare enough in public life to be considered a precious commodity to be treasured and preserved, not thrown to the prejudices of the crowd without support.

This kind of cooperation in the form of compromise is not always viewed as desirable. Indeed, at times, it is viewed as downright unfashionable.

Felix Rohatyn, the brilliant, tough-minded businessman, who did so much to save New York City in its time of crisis, said:

> *Commitment is not fashionable: cool is the order of the day ...*
> *we face the loss of our most precious assets all because we are*
> *cynical, self-indulgent and unwilling to make the effort.*

In short, we should recognize that what Niccolò Machiavelli observed long ago in the *Prince* continues to be a valid premise on which to proceed:

> *[T]here is nothing more difficult to take in hand, more perilous*
> *to conduct, or more uncertain in its success, than to take the*
> *lead in the introduction of a new order of things. Because the*
> *innovator has for enemies all those who have done well under*
> *the old conditions and lukewarm defenders in those who may do*
> *well under the new. This coolness arises partly from the fear of*
> *opponents, who have the laws on their side, and partly from the*
> *incredulity of men, who do not readily believe in the new things*
> *until they have long experienced them.*

For these reasons, the resolution of the great social issues today and tomorrow will not be found by those who are content with today and, therefore, are guided solely by polling and focus groups in their decision-making so as to reap the maximum short-term political benefit.

These issues will also not be effectively addressed by politicians who are apathetic toward the problem and their fellow human beings, or timid and fearful in the face of new ideas and bold projects. Rather, it will belong to those who can blend passion, reason, courage, and, perhaps, the patience to sustain a personal commitment to ideals that may not be reached or even visible in their lifetime.

How do we identify these leadership qualities in a candidate for public office? We focus far more on their record and, most importantly, their reputation among their peers and in their communities for being able "to get things done" if they are incumbents. If they are not, we focus on their positions on issues to see if they are logical and substantive as opposed to rigid and ideological.

At the risk of bringing on a charge of heresy from certain advocacy groups, I think a hard look for these qualities of character and temperament is infinitely more important than a candidate's position on individual issues.

PART THREE

Political Economics (Graduate Level)

Chapter 18

The Great Risk Shift

*"[W]e have witnessed a massive transfer of economic
risk from broad structures of insurance ... onto the
fragile balance sheets of American families."*

What are the big issues in 2010? And, more importantly, how should they be framed? One of the "big issues" if not "the biggest issue" is described in *The Great Risk Shift*, a book by Jacob S. Hacker, a political science professor at Yale University.

In his book, Hacker evokes a general theme, which is summarized in a single sentence:

> *Over the last generation ... we have witnessed a massive transfer of economic risk from broad structures of insurance, including those sponsored by the corporate sector as well as by government, onto the fragile balance sheets of American families.*

For evidence to support that proposition and theme, Hacker cites with clear opprobrium the growing volatility of family and individual incomes, escalating bankruptcies, and foreclosure rates; the collapse of defined-benefit corporate pensions; and the swelling ranks of Americans without health insurance, which he collectively describes as the consequences of "America's sweeping transformation away from an all-in-the-same boat philosophy of shared risk toward a go-it-alone vision of personal responsibility."

Hacker then attributes this transformation to the "Personal Responsibility Crusade," which has previously been labeled by others with less emphasis on its negative effects as "Reaganomics" or "The Opportunity Society."

In fact, this exact same historical trend, which is described by Jacob Hacker in arguably apocryphal terms, is welcomed by Brink Lindsay, vice president for research at the Cato Institute and author of *The Uncertain Struggle for Global Capitalism*, when he joyfully proclaims:

> *Out of the stagflation and malaise of the 1970s emerged a new and improved American economic system – less regulated and unionized, more globalized and entrepreneurial than the old triumvirate of Big Government, Big Business, and Big Labor that preceded it.*

Lindsay then summarily sweeps aside Hacker's writing and concerns by attributing them to the general reaction of the "political left," which, ever since the advent of "the improved American economic system" described as Reaganomics in the 1980s, has devoted a considerable portion of its intellectual energy to poor mouthing the ensuing prosperity.

While Lindsay sees the rapid rise of 401(K) plans, the creation of "health savings accounts," and the proposal to replace traditional Social Security benefits with "personal retirement accounts" as positive developments of the new and "improved" "entrepreneurial American economy" designed to replace tired and worn-out institutions and a malaise-infected culture, "which are reducing the level of our prosperity," Hacker sees these exact same trends as unfairly and, in this election year, unwisely shifting economic risk to families and individuals of their physical and mental health as well as their economic security at a cost they cannot afford.

Lindsay of the "Libertarian Right" candidly acknowledges that Hacker of "The Political Left" is correct in reaching his factual conclusion that intensified competitive pressures have increased the tempo of what Lindsay refers to as "creative destruction." That is, "turnover in the ranks of Fortune 500 companies and elsewhere have accelerated, and layoff rates (especially for white-collar workers) are up." Significantly, Lindsay further concedes that if what he labels as economic security "means security from potentially disruptive change, we probably do have less of it than before."

It strikes this writer that the use of the term "creative destruction," which Lindsay does not hesitate to use to describe people losing their jobs, fearing the loss of their jobs, as well as their confidence about their economic future and that of their families, is considerably more "slippery" then the term "economic security," which about as accurately as the English language permits describes those same acts and anxieties.

In any case, the shift of these risks, and the costs of that shift, to the health, welfare, and security of individuals and their families is real and deeply felt no matter what words we use to describe them.

The political issue is, then, what is the tradeoff? What benefit do individual citizens and their families receive in return for accepting (with their votes) "The Great Risk Shift" and enduring the additional economic insecurities and anxieties that have accompanied it during the last 28 years? The shift results from the policies of all but the eight years of the Clinton presidency, which arguably interrupted/paused the shift or at least slowed it from 1992 to 2000. The "Great Risk Shift" has been the public policy of all the Republican administrations during that period of time.

The resolution of this issue is not as clear as we might expect or even that we might desire. If the polls are correct, then after the last two elections in which the voters appeared to be concerned more with national security issues than with economic security issues, this election may be well decided by economic issues, including the "Great Risk Shift," which has taken place without any electoral scrutiny or even focus on it. That should change this year, barring another terrorist attack on the homeland.

As the issue develops, we will consider the full depth and breadth of the "trade-offs" between economic "security" and "prosperity."

What risks and trade-offs are associated with the policy status quo? Could it be a return to the pre-1980 era that Professor Jacob Hacker describes as an age of "economic stability and risk-sharing" as well as new markets and institutions for the 21st century we could develop, which could mitigate or even reduce some of the biggest risks faced by the American people?

These questions will certainly not be framed in this way for the debate, or for the paid political commercials aired by the candidates. But they should be answered directly.

Chapter 19

The Politics of the Shift of Economic Risk

*"You can always depend on the Americans to do the
right thing after they try everything else."*

What happens when interest-group politics gets out of control? Well, we're witnessing it, are we not faithful readers! Ironically, the most interesting analysis of what we're observing is arguably provided by a contemporaneous reading of and reflection on the messages of two books that I have written about previously in this space. Those books are, *The Process of Government: A Study of Social Pressures*, by Arthur Fisher Bentley published over 100 years ago (1908), and *The Great Risk Shift* by Yale University political science professor, Jacob S. Hacker.

As Nicholas Lemann, a "critic-at-large" for *The New Yorker* magazine, has pointed out:

> The Process of Government *is a 'hedgehog' of a book. Its point can be stated quite simply: 'All politics and all government are the results of the activities of groups.'*

What has changed dramatically in the last few years is the nature of the groups, who are now much more visibly and audibly dominating our politics. Those groups include the Tea Party organizations and other groups whose tactics and goals are very different from the organizations that helped create them by financing their growth.

These groups have as their goal the acceleration of the process of shifting economic risk described by Professor Jacob S. Hacker in his book. Hacker in 2008 cited as evidence of the shift a litany of deteriorating economic symptoms that plague the "recovery" we continue to wish for but so far don't see in 2011: the growing volatility of family and individual incomes; escalating bankruptcies and foreclosure rates; the collapse of defined-benefit governmental and corporate pensions; and the attempt to abolish the recently legislated mandate to provide health insurance to all Americans.

These trends are spun positively to the conservative base based on the need to balance the budget, economic philosophy, and freedom of choice. These themes resound even more effectively in 2011 than they did in 2008.

These trends are spun quite differently by Professor Hacker in his book. In fact, they are presented in almost apocryphal terms. They are, however, welcomed in the Tea Party circles—and by other groups and organizations whose birth during the Obama administration was at least partially occasioned by the arguably reasonable political perception of such respected organizations, such as the U.S. Chamber of Commerce, the Business Roundtable, and the National Association of Manufacturers, that a political rebalancing was necessary in light of the politics and policies of President Obama and an all Democratic Congress during the first two years of his administration.

The legislative products of those years included universally mandated health insurance (The Affordable Care Act); and the "Stimulus," which notwithstanding their recent rhetorical protests was embraced by most of corporate America, particularly when it served to bail out their members whose snail-mail addresses are "Wall Street, New York, NY."

The Dodd-Frank financial regulation bill was the last piece of comprehensive legislation aimed at the root causes of the recession, which may be officially over but is still being felt by most Americans. This recession and the legislative attempts to escape it simply highlight the unmistakable fact that the shifting of economic risk has been successfully undertaken. Dodd-Frank was and is not so much an attempt to shift risk back to the corporate sector as it is to reduce it quantitatively by regulating it.

To say all of this was unwelcome in corporate headquarters, and by extension their political stepchildren in the conservative base, is an understatement. In fact, it is not an exaggeration to suggest, as *Washington Post* op/ed. financial columnist Steven Pearlstein has, that it precipitated a "jihad against all regulation, all taxes, and all government" not by corporate America itself, but by right-wing zealots inadvertently created and financed by them.

How and why did this happen? More importantly, how did the U.S. Chamber of Commerce, the Business Roundtable, and the National Association of Manufacturers and their individual and corporate members lose control of their own political progeny and their agenda so completely?

Finally, what should "WE" do about rebalancing the allocation of political common sense, economic growth, and fairness (risk) on both sides of the aisle? Let us remember that Winston Churchill optimistically and non-categorically stated:

> *You can always depend on the Americans to do the right thing after they try everything else.*

Well, we're in the process of "trying everything else" so we've got time to figure out what the "right thing to do is."

Chapter 20

Corporate Networks, Power, and Money Precipitate Crisis of the Old Order

"It seems best to me to go straight to the actual truth of things rather than to dwell in dreams."

The effects of the recession have lingered on for everyone who hasn't benefited from what financial op/ed. columnist Steven Pearlstein describes as "the financialization of the U.S. economy." Financialization of the economy, and the excessive risk-taking associated with it, takes place when the "interests of its stockholders" (really The Management Class) become the single-minded focus of large corporations to the virtual exclusion of the interests of customers, employees, and society at large. This process that columnist Dana Wilbank alternatively describes as "revving up the engine of influence" has often been lamented as "the price we pay for living in our brand of democracy."

Perhaps, it is no more complicated than that!

The groups that are largely driving our broken politics are precipitating what economist Robert J. Samuelson characterizes as a "crisis of the old 'economic' order." Allan Sloane, senior editor-at-large of *Fortune* magazine, who describes himself as "an angry moderate who has finally gotten fed up with the lunacy and incompetence of our alleged national leaders," suggests that this crisis is caused by "knuckleheaded politicians driving us into a ditch."

These "knuckleheaded politicians" were born as a result of the union of money, networks, and power of such respected organizations as the U.S. Chamber of Commerce, the National Association of Manufacturers, and the Business Roundtable. They, in turn, created other organizations with such innocent-sounding names as Americans for a Sound Economy, Crossroads, Freedom Works, The Taxpayer League, etc.

Those organizations—with their ability to access clever and skilled lawyers and the financial resources to pay them along with a U.S. Supreme Court majority, which in the face of 40 years of precedent to the contrary now holds that "corporations are persons"—enabled them to enjoy some threshold success in attaining what were then limited goals of minimally reducing corporate tax rates and reducing or at least pushing back against some arguably burdensome and unnecessary regulations, as well as some meddlesome regulators whose judgment was lacking and/or who were incapable of applying a rigorous cost-benefit analysis to their work.

Somehow, somewhere, the backing of these organizations extended to candidates and organizations whose platforms were thought to thrust toward "limited government" and morphed into backing for what Sloane characterizes as "knuckleheaded" politicians and political organizations who as a result of a strange combination of zealotry and naiveté, interpreted this support as a license if not a mandate to abolish all regulation, all taxes, and most government.

This would include in varying degrees (which can be verified by watching the Republican debates and the work of Congress), the privatization of public schools; cutting back on basic research on which manufacturers base their product development; shutting down regulatory agencies that protect the public from dangerous products as well as businesses from unscrupulous competitors; and the privatization of the public infrastructure that transports our supplies and finished goods, among other things.

This modern-day nihilism at the federal level, which is on display daily in Washington, hopefully will not prove to be contagious and infect the states. Its symptoms can be spotted early and easily.

There is a massive loss of memory that is either brought on by a collective case of political and economic amnesia or a reaction to some food or medicine ingested recently, which causes delusional or hallucinatory ramblings, that the financial crises of 2008 were a dream like the season of the long-running soap opera, *Dallas*—which turned out to be a season-long dream.

In 2008, was it a dream (or nightmare)? Subprime mortgages? Too-big-to-fail banks? Unregulated derivatives? Not a problem ... didn't happen! Indeed, the crises of 2008 never happened and nothing needs to be done to prevent them from happening again.

This, of course, is not a dream but the nightmare we are in, which was created with flowing corporate dollars financing right-wing zealots who are not interested in advice or direction from the corporate interests who made their careers possible. There is still a way to get their attention, however. As the ultimate political philosopher, Niccolò Machiavelli, said a long time ago:

> *It seems best to me to go straight to the actual truth of things rather than to dwell in dreams.*

When the right-wing zealots who were elected using dollars that corporate America gave them to protect their limited interests run out of that money, cut them off until they begin to act responsibly and recognize that they cannot ignore their non-heavenly creators with impunity.

Chapter 21

Planning for Justice After the Revolution

> *"[E]very form of personal authority by which social control has ... been exercised has been weakened and replaced ... by a form of bureaucratic regulation."*

Bernie Sanders and Steve Bannon meet at the local bar, the visual of which resembles the television sitcom, *Cheers*, to talk about "what we have in common."

"We need a Political Revolution," Bernie repeats as he did so often during his 2016 campaign and thereafter.

We are in a "war against The Establishment" and the "Deconstruction of the Administrative State," says Steve, echoing his Breitbart-inspired refrain, which he reiterates without fear of getting more attention than his former boss since he departed the White House.

"Be careful what you ask for, you may already have it," replies Theodore Caplow, posing as a wise-in-the-ways-of-the-world bartender, who is a former world-renowned sociologist and author, bartending to have some fun in his later years and try his sociological theories and observations out on the Bernies and Steves of the world.

There is no evidence that this meeting ever took place. But there is ample evidence that it could have occurred.

Particularly in the last year, the world has, at times, seemed to be spinning on its axis and emitting rapid changes, which are not as geographically or culturally confined as they once were. Equally significant and noticeable is that the pace of these changes does not seem to be coordinated or even controllable by governments, "establishments," "elites," or any other human-made organization or entity.

Evidence of this trend just in the last few months and weeks includes the back and forth between the governments and the leaders of North Korea and the United States, with at least the appearance of a disconnect between the president of the United States and his secretary of state, and even between the president's Twitter feed and the writer of his speeches delivered during his travels in Asia.

This, coupled with the dynamic of women coming forward on a large scale almost daily, disclosing sexual assaults and harassment taking place as far back as 40 years ago (traumatic for Roy Moore, Harvey Weinstein, Senator Al Franken, and other heretofore protected, alleged sexual predators and harassers).

These daily "late-breaking news" events, along with the continuing multiple investigations of Russian interference in the U.S. and other western nations' elections by Special Counsel Robert Mueller and various congressional subcommittees serve to create the impression of events moving too fast on too many fronts to control.

Whether these events are described as a "political revolution" and/or a "War against the Establishment," they are constantly and inevitably injected into our daily lives by cable news, talk radio, and the internet. If these events and their coverage—individually, collectively, or cumulatively—cause any of us anxiety, it may be because the level of certainty and predictability we desire in our lives is routinely electronically shattered every day.

"The World is Flat," announced columnist and author Thomas L. Friedman in his book of the same name published in 2005. In that book, Friedman described the dramatic effect of what he labeled "Globalization 3.0" on the "newfound power of individuals to collaborate and compete globally." Friedman then explained that "individuals must and can now ask, 'where do I fit into the global competition and opportunities of the day, and how can I, on my own, collaborate with others globally?'"

In turn, this increased power of individuals, particularly women, has produced several societal trends that the eminent sociologist, Theodore Caplow, noted in his book, *American Social Trends*, first published in the 1990s. These trends have obviously accelerated in the 21st century.

The most discussed and probably the most dramatic was, and continues to be, the movement of women into the labor force. This trend was emphasized in the report, "A Woman's Nation Changes Everything" a/k/a "The Shriver Report," jointly produced and edited by the Center for American Progress and Maria Shriver. That report noted that married women are now the breadwinners in a majority of American families even though they still do not earn equal pay for equal work.

This trend is contemporaneous with other trends including the legitimization of unmarried consensual unions of both opposite and same-sex couples, a sharp decline in fertility, the reduction of paternal responsibilities, and the increase and diversification of those responsibilities in others, as well as a massive shift from blue-collar to white-collar employment.

Caplow characterized these changes as "transformative" and goes on to describe the events that led up to them as "a revolution against society rather than against the state." Caplow observed that:

> *"[E]very form of personal authority by which social control has in the past been exercised has been weakened and replaced at least in part by a form of bureaucratic regulation 'in the Twenty-First Century.'*

That "revolution against society" and the accompanying weakening of every form of personal authority by which social control has been exercised and maintained mostly by men in the past, in the opinion of this writer, directly accounts for the comparatively recent and sudden willingness of women to now come forward to report sexual harassment.

They previously did not disclose these incidents for fear of the repercussions on their jobs and careers over which mostly males had the unchecked authority to administer in almost every industry and most of government until recently.

The fact that this authority has been atrophying in the face of increased media scrutiny and replaced by external and internal bureaucratic regulation has not, until recently, been noticed by many women who were too busy multi-tasking in their daily lives to observe it. Now that the media has highlighted it, the complaints will likely increase exponentially as the culture change accelerates.

This observation is demonstrably true. Among the relationships clearly altered for better or worse, depending on your perspective, are those between managers and workers, men and women, parents and children, teachers and students, clergy and parishioners, as well as politicians and electorates.

Even the most authoritarian relationships, which Caplow concludes can still be found among physicians and patients and judges and litigants, are increasingly regulated by third parties and constrained by bureaucratic regulations. We see this in the enhanced regulatory and disciplinary authorities and regimens regulating lawyers and judges, as well as the increased "access to justice" accorded to our citizens, many of whom can now be seen and heard representing themselves in and out of our courthouses.

What this means, says 76-year-old scholar Theodore Caplow, is that institutions with reduced authority must be managed more skillfully than those that still have stronger internal authority. That means the judicial branch of government can no longer efficiently manage its limited resources, and those of its supporting agencies and staffs, by reacting to societal trends and developments rather than planning for them.

It means that the leaders of the justice system must accept the need for the same transformation and organizational change that is well advanced in many other private institutions all around us. This includes specialization and multi-disciplinary collaboration.

The managers and judges of the judicial branch of government should institutionalize the means to continuously recognize and research present and future societal trends and then plan for the impact on the courts. In doing so, judges and lawyers should recognize that we do not have exclusive right, title, and interest to the expertise to fairly and efficiently resolve all of our fellow citizens' disputes, and that consequently, justice is not to be found exclusively in our state and federal courtrooms or obtained after costly and time-consuming litigation.

Most of our citizens want access to justice regardless of where they have to go to get it. We should begin to plan for them to have access to justice quicker and easier than they do today, and we should not in the future restrict its availability only to courtrooms or even courthouses.

As we progress through the 21st century, those who will be leading the judicial branch of government must recognize that its mission is to serve justice by providing a comprehensive and diverse public dispute-resolution service, which is capable of resolving disputes fairly and efficiently and in a manner that enables the resolution of the dispute to be final and enforceable within a reasonable time.

This is more than a trial service. It is a conflict resolution service.

Chapter 22

Responsibility and Accountability in the Criminal Justice System: A Challenge

"We are all ... responsible and accountable for electing leaders, who will work together to produce a law enforcement system that is coordinated, efficient, and economical."

An important issue that we ought to pay attention to when we select our leaders in November is how they plan to ensure efficiency by insisting on responsibility and accountability in the criminal justice system. This debate is taking place in the form of countercharges by the two major party candidates for governor in their paid political advertising and in statements to the media. The issue being discussed is whether Mayor Martin O'Malley's policy of "zero tolerance" of "quality of life crimes" in Baltimore City is efficient and wise.

It is contended by Governor Robert Ehrlich and his spokesman on this issue, attorney and former Circuit Court Judge William Murphy, that this policy of the Baltimore City Police Department and Mayor O'Malley has resulted in "mass arrests" of individuals in Baltimore

City for allegedly committing "minor" or "quality of life crimes," *e.g.*, "loitering," disorderly conduct," "drunk in public," "malicious destruction of property– *i.e.*, graffiti," "petty theft," etc.

It is further pointed out by the critics of this policy that a disproportionate percentage of those persons arrested for these offenses are African American or other minority citizens. Following their arrests, these individuals are either never formally charged or the charges against them are summarily "dropped," meaning they are not prosecuted.

Although it is not mentioned in their paid political advertising, it is conceded that this policy has resulted in a substantial reduction in crime in Baltimore City. However, as far as its critics are concerned, the "substantial reduction in crime" is not enough to justify the large percentage of arrests that are not followed by formal prosecution.

There is no mention in any of the governor's ads about any positive effects of the policy, specifically the reduction of crime that has occurred contemporaneously and, therefore, arguably because of the policy. Conversely, the mayor's ads tout the reduction of crime in Baltimore without mentioning the downside of the policy, *i.e.*, the large number of arrests that are subsequently deemed to not be worthy of prosecution and, therefore, perhaps of dubious legality.

Now, I am not naive. I managed state and local political campaigns several lives ago before I became a judge and stopped having partisan thoughts. I realize that the purpose of paid political advertising is to persuade targeted voters to vote for the candidate paying for the 30– or 60-second spot, not to present a balanced or even complete view on an issue or societal problem.

Having acknowledged that, I will use the rest of my space in this column to comment further on how this debate can be developed into something more useful than a "get out the vote" technique.

First, some further truths to complement both candidates' advertising. The "zero tolerance" of "quality of life crime" is a law enforcement strategy that seeks to reduce all crime by not tolerating any crime. It has worked in one form or another in other cities, such as New York, Boston, and Philadelphia, as well as in Baltimore. In all those cities, as in Baltimore, the same criticisms have been made.

The policy is made even more controversial than it would be otherwise by the fact that this law enforcement strategy is not shared by Baltimore City State's Attorney Patricia Jessamy, who is independently elected and who, in the criminal justice system, has the exclusive and final say over whether a person arrested will be prosecuted.

Baltimore City State's Attorney Jessamy and her assistant state's attorneys choose not to prosecute many of the people arrested for these "quality of life crimes" for a variety of reasons, including a cost-benefit analysis. This cost-benefit analysis begins and, in many cases, ends with the fact that, even though technically the case could be successfully prosecuted, it is not worth it because the arrest itself deters further criminal activity by the suspect, which is the only purpose for detaining the person even briefly.

The police know that, in many cases, the State's Attorney's Office will not prosecute individuals arrested for these "minor" crimes. That being the case, the critics of this policy suggest that the mayor and his police department are violating the civil rights of certain citizens, particularly identifiable minority citizens, ostensibly to make other citizens safer by preventing crime.

The critics then question whether it should continue. The question that the governor and his spokesman, Mr. Murphy, do not answer in their political ad is, "Are they willing to trade off the reduced crime rate and the improved quality of life that accompanies it to return crime to the levels that made the City more dangerous prior to Martin O'Malley becoming Mayor?" The governor should answer this question if he wants this policy to be an issue in this election.

This hammer, of course, should swing both ways. Does the mayor believe that arresting large numbers of minority citizens, who are then not prosecuted for the alleged minor crimes committed because under any cost-benefit analysis it makes no sense, is a legally acceptable and appropriate law enforcement strategy because crime is deterred even if not punished by this process?

If so, is there a quantitative or qualitative "tipping point" where these arrests become abusive and, therefore, intolerable? That question is never addressed in any of the mayor's political ads. The mayor should answer this question if he wants credit for the reduction in Baltimore's crime rate to be a reason to elect him governor.

Finally, we may want to ask the mayor, the governor, and the independently elected state's attorney whether any of them think not having a joint law enforcement strategy on this, as well as in other areas, is in the interest of the citizens of Baltimore and the state of Maryland?

Do the governor, the mayor, and the state's attorney believe that the criminal justice system can ever hope to work efficiently if the law enforcement strategy of the independently elected state's attorney is not coordinated with that of the police department?

Their collective and individual answers to these questions logically must be, "Of Course Not!" If so, then the next questions to the governor, mayor, and state's attorney must be:

- "If you wish to be elected or re-elected, don't you think in your current or new office that you have a responsibility to move beyond your electoral posturing and targeting voters to devise an effective and coordinated law enforcement strategy that will work for all of the people?"

- "Do you favor a law enforcement strategy that will be synergistic instead of disjointed?"

- "Is law enforcement enhanced by a strategy that is uncoordinated?"

- "Doesn't this political and other criticism visibly undermine public trust, confidence, and respect for law enforcement and the courts?"

The overriding principle of accountability in the criminal justice system is not confined to governors, mayors, and state's attorneys. Judges, collectively and individually, should be willing to accept responsibility for their decisions and to be held accountable by the media, victims, the citizens of his or her jurisdiction, as well as the accused.

That means that when a judge makes a decision to exclude, or what lawyers and judges refer to as "suppress," otherwise reliable evidence of a crime from a trial because it was obtained in the judge's view in violation of the constitutional rights of the accused or not presented as the law requires, that judge should explain the basis for that ruling and should not blame others for his or her decision.

The judge should also explain, if it is not obvious, the constitutional and statutory provisions or "rule" that requires the judge's decision be what it is and, if necessary and appropriate, defend rather than attack the wisdom of the law and the balancing of the need for order and liberty, which caused it to be enacted.

More importantly, when a judge exercises his or her discretion, most often evident in decisions relating to whether to release an accused until his or her trial and in sentencing convicted criminal defendants, he or she should be prepared to explain, defend, and be held accountable for those decisions.

Judges should recognize and acknowledge that all media coverage and scrutiny of their decisions, as well as proposals for judicial evaluations, are not threats to judicial independence and should not be considered as such.

Any judge who comes to the Bench thinking that he or she should be immune, or otherwise shielded from criticism, should begin looking for some other line of work and should probably give up his or her day job while conducting the search.

Ironically, defense attorneys in our system are not publicly accountable in the same way judges and prosecutors are. Nor should they be. Defense attorneys are certainly responsible as Officers of the Court and accountable for fully complying with the letter and the spirit of the Rules of Professional Conduct, which include important provisions requiring an attorney to proceed in good faith at all times and to always be candid with the court and with other counsel, including prosecutors.

However, with this very significant limitation or qualification, a criminal defense attorney's primary duty and responsibility is to defend and counsel his or her client zealously. A criminal defense attorney is not accountable to the general public. His or her duty to defend a client does not depend to a degree on what his or her client is charged with or how horrible the client's conduct is alleged or perceived to be.

We are all, however, responsible and accountable for electing leaders, who will work together to produce a law enforcement system that is coordinated, efficient, and economical. This principle should shape our debate.

It has not done so to date.

Chapter 23

New Era for International Courts and the United States

*"[I]t is not law that needs to be protected from politics,
but politics from law."*

The New Year approaches with even more "new beginnings" than usual on the horizon. A new president of the United States and with him a new administration, for whom the latest polls have shown the people have great hopes and expectations, will take office within the first three weeks of the New Year.

If the media coverage and analysis is accurate, the approach of the new administration to issues will be less ideological and more pragmatic than its predecessor. The now fully selected cabinet leaders and White House staff consist of, in the words of more than one commentator, "smart, strong," and in some cases already "outsized personalities" recognized on the world stage, who will be called upon in short order to shape a new global economic and geopolitical world order.

President-Elect Barack Obama obviously is not intellectually insecure, timid, or indecisive in the presence of strong, smart, competent people. Indeed, he apparently sees the inevitable debate among them on important national security and world economic issues as an essential prerequisite to ensuring the quality of his decision-making processes. Hopefully, high-quality decisions will result from unfiltered information and opinions on all sides of these issues being thoroughly presented and considered before being resolved by the president.

This is particularly important in the development of the U.S. policy on the role of International Law and International Courts. As I noted in a previous column, during my recent visit to The Hague, Netherlands, where many of these international tribunals and other organizations are located, I noticed that judges and court administrators are both idealistic and realistic even in the face of U.S. skepticism about their role and value.

In fact, as Daniel Terris, Cesare P.R. Romano, and Leigh Swigert point out in their pioneering study of the international judiciary in their book, *The International Judge*:

> *They are surprisingly patient and philosophical about U.S. objections taking a long view that stretches into the past and future* [because they recognize that] *when it comes to the intersection of international law and politics, no issue is more important or more sensitive than the role of the United States.*

Unfortunately, as Terris, Romano, and Swigert illustrate in their book, the recent hostility to not only specific decisions of international courts but to the very idea of international law itself, which predated the George W. Bush administration but without question intensified during the last eight years, "poses a significant threat to the effectiveness of justice on a global scale." It is not difficult to figure out why.

The rule of law depends on public trust and confidence in the judiciary. Therefore, while judges' real independence from political prejudices and pressure is vital, it is equally or perhaps even more important that the judges' independence be perceived and understood clearly. This is even more important for international judges and their courts than for domestic judges.

The independence of international courts and judges is much more suspect because the very legitimacy of international law itself is still a matter of serious debate.

The debate over the legitimacy of "international law" is very real. It is ongoing and not without intellectual foundation. It should not, therefore, be dismissed or ignored. Rather, all side of the debate should be reexamined carefully and respectfully, but not in an ideological straight jacket or vacuum. Those who favor the application of international law through international tribunals should get equal time and consideration.

Critics of the application of international law to parties limited by a well-defined jurisdictional rule continue to sound the rhetorical and policy alarm bell when it is suggested that international law be applied to all—even in limited circumstances.

Former federal Judge Robert Bork says, "International law is not law, but politics." He then goes on to explain:

> *For that reason, it is dangerous to give the name 'law' which summons up respect to political struggles that are essentially lawless.*

Former Secretary of State Henry Kissinger reaches the same conclusion, but for opposite reasons. Kissinger says:

> *[I]t is not law that needs to be protected from politics, but politics from law, [warning that international adjudication] is being pushed to extremes which risk substituting the 'Tyranny of Judges' for that of governments.*

> *Far better to allow political matters to take their course in the arena of diplomacy or even conflict than to allow the intrusion of 'unaccountable judges' into the domain of diplomats.*

This criticism and these warnings have a familiar ring to them. They sound eerily like the usual right-wing diatribes against judges generally that have been heard in this country in every election that I can remember.

Their validity is dependent on a worldview, which presupposes that states and individuals act purely on the basis of power. If that world view is accepted, then as Terris, Romano, and Swigert concede, "International courts are at best frivolous and at worst destructive."

That world view, however, is clearly not universally reality-based. International courts have taken their place alongside a host of institutions that created or evolved from new and innovative forms of global politics, where nongovernmental actors work alongside powerful governments where at times symbolic action plays as prominent a role as military might; where persuasion can, and where governments have, evidenced a stake in reigning in their own excesses, if it also means reigning in the excesses of their former leaders, their neighbors, and enemies.

This new world and reality should not be ignored. The fact that the interdependence of our world is not yet fully recognized is not a reason for our country to refuse to consider resuming our historical role as an advocate for international courts with binding authority.

President William Howard Taft, not exactly a great liberal, called for an international court in 1910 as "a better method of settling controversies than war." President Theodore Roosevelt, not exactly a left-wing pacifist, hailed "the great advance which the world is making toward the substitution of the rule of reason and justice for simple force."

President-Elect Barack Obama should follow in their visionary footsteps with his usual eloquence—and what appears so far to be his almost equally impressive organizational skills—to point out to the citizens of the United States and the world that "when idealistic principals are wholesale surrendered to realistic politics, humanity becomes the victim."

Let us all hope for peace on earth, goodwill to all beginning in 2009 through the application of international law.

Happy New Year!

Older and Wiser

"A sense of humor is just common-sense dancing.
Those who lack humor are without judgment and
should be trusted with nothing."

My first book, *Lessons Lived & Learned: My Life On and Off the Bench*, describes my journey through a public and private life, including memorable characters I have met, been mentored by, and experienced, along with the lessons learned from those individuals. Those persons include elected and appointed officials and political leaders, lawyers, and judges, as well as some colorful rogues and scoundrels.

Lessons Lived & Learned documents and explains my life's journey, the experiences and the people who guided me, detoured me, and made my stops and starts interesting—and at times, entertaining.

These "lessons learned" are presented in the context of a deep sense of humility developed over a period of time beginning in my ascendant teenage years, self-centered 20s, and even 30s and 40s when I was focused on climbing the perceived mountain of outward success and professional achievement that ultimately led to a successful law practice and three judgeships.

That road briefly descended in my 50s to a quietly disquieting personal valley of mid-life divorce and doubt for a short period of time. That time was comparatively brief, although it provided an intense learning experience that resulted in a much greater appreciation for the meaning of life, the value of the love of my children, grandchildren, friends, and family—even my ex-wife.

Later, in my 60s and now in my 70s, I am convinced that I am both older and wiser. Marc Freedman, chief executive at Encore.org and author of *How to Live Forever: The Enduring Power of Connecting the Generations*, documents the following conclusion:

> *There is a U-bend of happiness in life – on average, we're upbeat early on, then hit the skids in midlife before growing far happier later.*

That midlife skid is further explained by Jonathan Rauch, who points out that in our 50s, we can see the deficiencies of the first half of life, but haven't figured out the second half's imperatives, even though as Stanford psychologist Laura Carstensen explains, we realize that there are fewer years ahead than behind. This realization drives us to seek deeper connections than what we had previously with those we care about.

This book follows my first book for a very specific reason. In this book, I hope the older and wiser Steven Platt has been able to relate the lessons of his life's journey with the two big "Hs"—humility and humor.

The Australian-born writer, Clive James, wrote:

> *A sense of humor is just common-sense dancing. Those who lack humor are without judgment and should be trusted with nothing.*

I agree!

Most of the columns, blogs, and speeches included are about the people, institutions, relationships, commitments, and trust that I and others have relied on during our lifetimes. Particularly now, many of them appear to be failing and under attack.

They should be cherished, defended, and reinforced with all of their complexity intact. Arthur Brooks, president of The American Enterprise Institute and author of *Love Your Enemies: How Decent People Can Save America from the Culture of Contempt*, acknowledges that our problem in America is not as widely believed—incivility or intolerance.

Rather, it is as explained in a 2014 article in *The Proceedings of the National Academy of Sciences*, "Motive Attribution Asymmetry," the "assumption that your ideology is based in love and your opponent's is based on hate." The researchers found that the average Republican and the average Democrat suffer from a level of "motive attribution asymmetry" that is comparable with that of Palestinians and Israelis. That is, each side thinks it is driven by benevolence, while the other is evil and motivated by hatred, and is therefore an enemy with whom one cannot negotiate or compromise.

These positions are taken by people who have lost their sense of humor and any semblance of humility—or never had them to begin with. They need to either get them back or be replaced by people whose personal transformation has evolved to the extent that they can lead the necessary social transformation.

That evolution, to a certain extent, as columnist David Brooks points out, is a product of age—the stage of life when one has reached his or her 60s and is mature enough to recognize that contempt is, in the words of philosopher Arthur Schopenhauer, "the unsullied conviction of worthlessness of another" and is "a noxious brew of anger and disgust."

I believe this book reflects that I am both older and wiser. If that means my words can help rescue our relationships and institutions, my purpose will have been served.

Other Books by This Author

Black Robe Fever

The Role of the Judge in American Society

The Winding Road

Criminal Courts, Civil Matters, and the Ongoing Quest for Access to Justice

Lessons Lived & Learned

My Life On and Off the Bench

RAMSES HOUSE PUBLISHING LLC
BALTIMORE, MD

D

E

F

G

H

I

Q

R

S

T

U

W